LETTERS AND SERMONS

OF

BESA

CORPUS
SCRIPTORUM CHRISTIANORUM ORIENTALIUM
EDITUM CONSILIO
UNIVERSITATIS CATHOLICAE AMERICAE
ET UNIVERSITATIS CATHOLICAE LOVANIENSIS

Vol. 158

SCRIPTORES COPTICI
TOMUS 22

LETTERS AND SERMONS
OF
BESA

TRANSLATED
BY

K. H. KUHN

LOVANII
IN AEDIBUS PEETERS
1956

ISSN 0070-0428
ISBN 978-90-429-0192-6

Éditions Peeters, Bondgenotenlaan 153, B-3000 Louvain

INTRODUCTION

Besa did not achieve fame comparable to that of his famous predecessor, Shenoute, so a brief word of introduction should perhaps accompany this translation of his letters and sermons.

When Shenoute died, probably in A.D. 466 [1], Besa succeeded him as abbot of the White Monastery, near Sohâg in Upper Egypt. The date of Besa's death is unknown, but there is evidence which suggests that he must have lived at least until A.D. 474.

The manuscripts of the letters and sermons translated in this volume are listed in detail in the introduction to CSCO, 157/Copt.21, which contains the text.

By far the greatest part of the text is contained in the remains of two codices, Codex A and Codex B. These reconstructed codices are both written on parchment and may be dated in the VIIth-VIIIth and the VIIIth century respectively. The sequence of contents for a considerable part of the two codices seems to have been the same. I have therefore arranged the surviving portions of text in the order which must have been common to them both, drawing on whichever is extant.

The rest of the text is contained in the manuscripts C-I, ranging from seven complete folios to one damaged folio. They are all written on parchment and can be dated between the VIIth-Xth centuries.

The extent of text parallels, together with a full critical apparatus, is given in footnotes to the text, while in this volume only such variants as affect the translation are noted.

I have translated into modern English and eschewed the archaic forms of the second person. After careful consideration, I have decided to adhere to this principle also in the many biblical

[1] According to J. Leipoldt, *Schenute von Atripe*, Texte und Untersuchungen 25, 1, N.F. 10, 1, Leipzig, 1903, pp. 44 ff., Shenoute died in A.D. 451; but cf. J. F. Bethune-Baker, 'The date of the death of Nestorius: Schenute, Zacharias, Evagrius', in *The Journal of Theological Studies*, IX, pp. 601 ff.

quotations and allusions. My reason for so doing is to avoid disrupting the unity of Besa's writings, couched throughout as they are in a language impregnated with the biblical idiom.

In all references to the O.T. I have followed the numeration in the LXX (H. B. Swete, *The Old Testament in Greek*, Cambridge, 1887 ff.).

CODICES **A** AND **B**.

[Fragment 1] *ON VIGILANCE*

I. **1.** [why do you] subject [yourselves] to ordinances in the world as those who are alive, touch not, nor taste, nor go near?'[1] This means that we have departed from the sins of the world by having renounced them. Why do we again turn to be implicated in them?

II. **1.** On this it has also been said, 'For you at that time were darkness but now are light in the Lord : walk as children of the light — for the fruit of the light is in all goodness, and righteousness, and truth — examining what is pleasing to the Lord, and have no fellowship with the unfruitful works of darkness, but rather expose them. **2.** For the things they do stealthily are disgraceful even to mention. But all things are manifest which are exposed by the light, for all things which are manifest are light'[2]. **3.** Therefore, let us expose our follies in us and all the thoughts of the devil which he plants in us, and the disbeliefs, and hatreds, inasmuch as we are made to think evil against one another while we are not for one another at all. **4.** And we blame one another and not ourselves[3], as long as our fight is against one another and not against principalities and powers, against the world-rulers of the darkness, against the spiritual (armies) of wickedness under heaven, and (it should be a fight) not against blood and flesh[4]. **5.** Thus has the apostle said, 'Take to yourselves[5] the panoply of God that you may be able to stand up to the wiles of the devil because our fight is not against blood and flesh'[6].

III. **1.** So therefore, be watchful that we may embrace the good, for there are many who are with one another in the body but far from one another in heart and love. Furthermore there are many who, though not with one another in the body, are with one another always in the love of Christ, and the love of the Spirit, and the good-pleasure of Jesus. **2.** And you, brethren, be watchful and continue in the things we have * taught[7], and many shall learn and * p. 2

[1] Col. 2. 20-21. [2] Eph. 5. 8-13. [3] Cf. the quotation from Antony on p. 93 and p. 97. [4] Cf. Eph. 6. 12. [5] Eph. 6. 13. [6] Eph. 6. 11-12.
[7] According to my emendation; but perhaps the text should be translated : 'you have displayed'.

profit from you, even as it has been said, 'Let them see your good works and glorify your Father which is in heaven'[8]. **3.** For even as you have followed all the saints in your actions, as it has been said, 'But you followed my teaching, my example, my purpose, my faith, my long-suffering, my love, my patience, my persecutions, my sufferings'[9], follow them also by guarding for yourselves your sufferings. For those who have imperishable wealth in Christ ought to watch over it..

IV. **1.** If those who have property, gold and silver and possessions, watch lest robbers steal it; then how much more fitting is it for us to watch lest the enemy steal the good which we do — our prayers, and our fastings, and our purity, and our constancy. **2.** For the theft of silver and gold is not on the same level. But in proportion as virginity and the monastic way of life are precious, so is the enemy eager to steal them. He who has acquired for himself pearls or gold keeps vigil. If the enemy keeps vigil for the sake of wickedness, then how much more shall he who has property watch lest it be plotted for.

V. **1.** Let us remember what our father has said, 'Brethren of our way of life fast and pray too; they keep vigil, but they also lie, fight, quarrel, murmur, and speak evil. They hate, walk in disaffection, defile themselves, and are deceitful; they commit every evil deed. Such men labour in vain and no advantage at all shall accrue to them. Moreover their constancy is in vain'. **2.** As it has been said, 'A sheaf without the fulness to yield meal'[10]. On this it has also been said, 'Sow wheat and reap thorns. Their lots shall not profit them'[11]. **3.** Watch, therefore, do not let the enemy destroy the good which we do, but with all vigilance guard our hearts from every foul thought of the devil that we may be worthy to hear
* p. 3 * this with confidence, 'They shall not work for strangers from now on but they shall work for the Lord their God'[12].

VI. **1.** For robbers do not break into a house or place where there is no property, but they break into the place where property is to be found; and they do not break into the place which is guarded against despoiling, but the place where they know they do not

8 Cf. Mt. 5. 16. 9 II Tim. 3. 10-11. 10 Hos. 8. 7. 11 Jer. 12. 13.
12 Jer. 37. 8-9.

guard and are asleep, into such do they break and carry off whatever they find. **2.** Thus also, the devil does not rob him who is watchful and guards his suffering but him whom he shall find off his guard, who neither fears God nor remembers how he is to come into the hands of God. But he who is carried about with every wind[13], him he robs of the good which he does unsparingly.

VII. **1.** Therefore, brethren, everyone who is of one mind with God and with our fathers and with us also, whether man or woman, whether great or small, with us and with you, take courage and be vigilant. Do not give sleep to our eyes or slumber to our eyelids[14] until the Lord has delivered us from every temptation of the enemy. For many are they who envy us. **2.** And do not regard brethren who are often disturbed in fighting and quarrelling and who deny their constancy and offend you. But let God not say that they ever offend the godloving, who have their faith towards Christ perfected and abide with the Spirit of God.

VIII. **1.** But as for you who sin and renounce constancy and who disturb the communities with meanness of spirit, envy, hatred, fighting, quarrelling, and deceit, woe to you, what shall you do on the day of your visitation? For your affliction is coming from afar[15]. **2.** Or is it not a matter for condemnation for us that we — after having renounced what we have renounced, and having made an agreement with him with whom we have made an agreement in a vow promising[16] : we will not steal, we will not lie, we will not defile our body in any way, we will not bear false witness, we will not do anything deceitful secretly, and all the other words which come after these — that we turn again and do these things once more? ... *2 folios missing* ...

[Fragment 2] *EXHORTATIONS*

I. **1.** * [wo]rld, when we were walking in defilements, and drunken- * p. 4
nesses, and revellings, and carousals, and abominable idolatries[1], walking in wickedness and envy, hateful and hating one another[2],

13 Cf. Eph. 4. 14. 14 Cf. Prov. 6. 4. 15 Is. 10. 3. 16 Cf. the vow introduced by Shenoute, J. Leipoldt, *Sinuthii archimandritae vita et opera omnia*, Paris, CSCO, 42/Copt.2 (1908), p. 20, and 73/Copt.5 (1913), p. 40.

1 Cf. I Pet. 4. 3. 2 Tit. 3. 3.

disobedient, erring [3], walking in the vanity of our hearts, darkened in our thoughts, alienated from the life of God because of the ignorance which was in us and because of our obstinacy, having given ourselves up to defilement and the performance of every uncleanness. **2.** Now we were not taught in this manner [4] but rather thus were we taught, 'Work out your salvation in fear and trembling. For it is God who works in you the will and the fulfilment of the will' [5].

II. **1.** Moreover Moses, at that time, having seen how the children of Israel hastened to forget the commandments of God, commanded them to make fringes on the borders of their garments that they might see them and remember and not forget the commandments of God [6]. But as for us, let us put the fear of God into our hearts instead of fringes that we may not forget the commandments which our fathers have given us. **2**. Therefore, brethren, let us turn and repent before the opportunity has gone from us, and while the light is with us, which is the teachings of our fathers. As the Lord has said, 'Walk as long as you have the light, that the darkness may not overtake you' [7]. And, 'As being in the day, let us walk decently' [8]. And, 'For those who sleep sleep in the night, and those who are drunk are drunk in the night. But we are of the day. Let us be sober, having put upon us the breastplate of fa[ith] [9]

[Fragment 3] *ON THE PUNISHMENT OF SINNERS*

I. **1.** for ever, as it is written, 'The Lord has arisen like the sleeper, like a strong man drunk with wine. He has smitten his
* p. 5 enemies backwards, he has put them to reproach for ever' [1]. **2.** * For he who has said, 'I will trample with my shoe upon Edom' [2], has also said, 'Because you have defiled my holy things with all your abominations, I will cast you away, my eye will not spare you, and I will have no mercy [on you]' [3]. **3.** They waited for light, the darkness of their evil deeds befell them; and they awaited light, they walked in the darkness [of] their disobedience. They groped for the wall like a blind man, which means like those who have no understanding;

3 Cf. Tit. 3. 3. 4 Cf. Eph. 4. 17-20. 5 Phil. 2. 12-13. 6 Cf. Num. 15. 38-39. 7 Jn. 12. 35. 8 Rom. 13. 13. 9 I Thes. 5. 7-8.

1 Ps. 77. 65-66. 2 Ps. 107. 10. 3 Ez. 5. 11.

and they felt as do those who have no eyes, [and] they fell at noonday like those at midnight [4], which means like those who did not hear scripture and were never taught.

II. **1.** But you, my beloved, building yourselves up in your most holy faith, praying in the Holy Spirit, keep yourselves in the love of God, looking for the mercy of our Lord Jesus Christ unto eternal [life, and] dragging some out of the fire [5], which is their abominable works and their pestilent words, and with hatred hating the garment defiled by the flesh [6]. **2.** And beware lest you be led in the error of the lawless and fall from your steadfastness [7]. Do not be like those who walk deceitfully amongst us, be they men or women, who have not remembered what is written, 'Children who have been defiled are not of God' [8]. And, 'He who defiles the temple of God, him will God destroy, for the temple of God is holy, which is you. Let no one deceive himself' [9]. **3.** And do not be like those who hate the things of God, and who despise the ordinances and the works of salvation which Christ Jesus thus performs in his monasteries, for a ransom and confirmation of his sons and daughters who desire their salvation, as it is written, 'He has given a sign to those who fear him that they may flee from before the arrow [10], that your beloved may be saved' [11].

III. **1.** But as for these haters of good, the boasters who despise our fathers and the ordinances which they laid down for us, do not pay heed to them [and] their pestilent words [which they] speak, so that * the word which is written may be accomplished upon such * p. 6
people. **2.** As those who slander God said formerly, namely, 'Everyone who does evil is good in the sight of the Lord, and his good-pleasure is upon them' [12]; so is it now with these who are honouring those who do evil, and glorifying those who sin in the sight of God, but despising those who fear the Lord and tremble at his name. **3.** They turn judgement into gall and the fruit of righteousness into bitterness [13]. They count darkness for light and light for darkness; they also say of the bitter that it is sweet and of the sweet that it is bitter [14].

[4] Cf. Is. 59. 9-10. [5] Jude 20-22. [6] Jude 23. [7] II Pet. 3. 17. [8] I cannot identify this quotation. [9] I Cor. 3. 17-18. [10] Cf. Ps. 59. 6 [11] Ps. 59. 7. [12] Mal. 2. 17. [13] Cf. Amos 6. 12. [14] Cf. Is. 5. 20.

IV. **1.** 'For the fool', it has been said, 'will speak follies and his heart will devise inanities to accomplish lawlessnesses and to voice error against the Lord'[15]. **2.** For they have spoken iniquity towards the height; they have exalted their mouth unto heaven and their tongue has come forth from the earth[16]. They say, 'How has God known?', and, 'Has there been knowledge on high?' Behold, these are thriving sinners, they have grabbed their wealth for ever[17], which is their hypocrisy and their deceitful works. **3.** Therefore their pride has given them power. They have clothed themselves with their iniquity and their impiety. Their iniquity is coming forth as out of their fat; they have arrived at a plan in their hearts. They have considered and spoken evilly[18].

V. **1.** For each one of these wretched ones, doubting in their constancy, has spoken vanities with his neighbour[19] who is of like mind in evil-speaking and disaffection, saying, 'These things are not good which those who are troubled at heart over the lawlessnesses which have happened in their midst are doing', as it is written, 'Those who do not honour the assemblies abandon the counsels[20] and ordinances which are made in the name of God and his Christ'. **2.** Thus it has been said, 'Them that sin reprove in the sight of all, that the rest also may be in fear'[21]. But these people have said, 'It is not good to reprove them nor to do anything to them, but it is
* p. 7 fitting to send them away secretly so that they depart'. **3.** * These agents of destruction and these who incite God to anger, whether man or woman, who know neither the scriptures nor the power of God[21a] and who do not know the straight way but, being perverted, pervert others, according to the saying, 'But he who is perverted carries his destruction in his mouth'[22], (these) have also said, 'What have they to do with them? They have left; it was not fitting that they should be brought and should have these things done to them'.

VI. **1.** O senseless men, do you not know that it is not man who does these things to them but God, as it has been said, 'I will pay your recompense upon your heads'?[23] **2.** And, ' "If you do not lay it to your heart to give glory to my name", says the Lord, the

15 Is. 32. 6. 16 Ps. 72. 8-9. 17 Ps. 72. 11-12. 18 Ps. 72. 6-8. 19 Ps. 11. 3. 20 Prov. 15. 22. 21 I Tim. 5. 20. 21a Mt. 22. 29, Mk. 12. 24. 22 Prov. 16. 26. 23 Joel 3. 4, Joel 3. 7.

Almighty, "I will send the curse to you, and I will curse your blessing and scatter your blessing abroad, and it shall not be with you, because you do not lay it to your heart" '[24]. **3.** Thus also our holy father says in his grief, 'If we do not recognise of what sort we are, the blood of each one shall come again upon his head'.

VII. **1.** Again he says rebukingly, being angry with those who do these pestilent things[25], 'Is it not the place and the day wherein God shall destroy your souls and your bodies? And is it (not) the time? Not only will I cause the laws to scour your sides and let a fire be kindled beneath you and your heads be cut off, but I would also set up gallows in the streets of these communities and have you hanged on them until you dry up and the birds eat your flesh[26] which you have made members of deceit. And I would slay you with my hands even as the priests of Baal[27] because you were not priests in his[28] house fittingly but you rather destroyed it'.

VIII. **1.** 'For if God spared not the angels when they had sinned', as it is written, 'but cast them down to hell in endless darkness, having delivered them to be kept unto the day of judgement to be punished[29], and especially those who walked * after the flesh * p. 8
in the lust of defilement[30], and did not spare the ancient world but submerged them in a flood of water and wiped out the ungodly men, except one man who was saved with his household[31], how then shall we escape, having neglected so great a salvation?'[32] **2.** According to that which has been said, 'God did not call us unto defilement but in purity. So now, he who rejects was not rejecting man, but God, who gives his Holy Spirit to you'[33]. **3.** Shall we not then put away from us this senselessness, this shamelessness, this presumptuousness, and this boastfulness?

[24] Mal. 2. 2. [25] For the following quotation, cf. MS. Copte, No. 2, ⲥϥⲁ̄ (Institut français d'archéologie orientale, Cairo), an unedited Shenoute MS. which M. Ch. Kuentz, then director, kindly allowed me to consult. This quotation is difficult to translate. The context seems to demand that the first two clauses be questions, not irreal conditional clauses. This use of ⲉⲛⲉⲣⲉ-, however, is not attested in the grammars. In the translation I have assumed that the two future imperfects, ⲛⲉⲓ̈ⲛⲁⲧⲁϩⲟ and ⲛⲉⲓ̈ⲛⲁⲕⲱⲛⲥ̄, are dependent on an unexpressed protasis (e.g. 'if it were necessary'). [26] Cf. Gen. 40. 19. [27] Cf. III Kg. 18. 40. [28] I.e. God's. [29] Cf. II Pet. 2. 4. [30] II Pet. 2. 10. [31] Cf. II Pet. 2. 5. [32] Heb. 2. 3. [33] I Thes. 4. 7-8.

IX. **1.** Be taught, O brethren, be taught. Do not let us be without fear. Remember the things we read, 'It is a fearful thing to come into the hands of the living God'[34]; and again, 'It is a fearful thing to expect the judgement and the fierceness[35] of the fire which will devour the adversaries'[36]. Remember also that it has been said, 'Let fear and trembling take hold of all[37], that the fire of Gehenna may not take hold of them'. **2.** Now therefore brethren, whether man or woman, let us depart from these evil things and these provocations of God to anger, lest we repent at our end. **3.** Someone has said somewhere, 'He who does not look forward to the place of judgement, does not establish his character'; and, 'He who does not look forward to the crown, is not constant'[38]. **4.** Moreover someone else has said elsewhere[39], 'Behold, brethren, we have seen from the holy scriptures that those who follow the will of God shall inherit his good things, as it is written, "There is an inheritance for those who serve the Lord"[40], **5.** but those who follow after the evil will of their hearts are ripe for wrath, as it has been said, "Their worm shall not die and their worm[41] shall not be quenched and they shall be for all flesh to see them"'[42].

* p. 9 X. **1.** * But as for us, let us reverence these sayings, and depart from these evil aspirations which war against us, lest we make ourselves sorrowful on the day of judgement, the day when God shall judge the world in righteousness and the people in his truth[43], the day which is a sentence, completing and cutting short, which God will execute upon the earth[44]. **2.** For the day of the Lord was appointed to be bitter, harsh, and powerful[45]. A day of wrath is that day; it is a day of tribulation and anguish[46]. It is a day of shouting and the trumpet[47]; it is a day of grief and sighing for those who have not prepared their works well for the way[48], which

[34] Heb. 10. 31. [35] This agrees with the Greek ζῆλος against the Sah. N.T. (cf. *The Coptic Version of the New Testament in the Southern Dialect*, Oxford, 1911-1924; and *The Coptic Version of the Acts of the Apostles and the Pauline Epistles in the Sahidic Dialect*, ed. H. THOMPSON, Cambridge, 1932) which has ⲕⲱϩⲧ 'flame', an obvious corruption. [36] Heb. 10. 27. [37] Cf. perhaps Ex. 15. 16. [38] Cf. Zech. 6. 14. [39] For the following quotation, cf. p. 74. [40] Is. 54. 17. [41] Obviously in error for : 'fire'. [42] Is. 66. 24. [43] Ps. 95. 13. [44] Rom. 9. 28. [45] Cf. Zeph. 1. 14. [46] Zeph. 1. 15. [47] Cf. Zeph. 1. 16. [48] Cf. Prov. 24. 42.

means for their departure out of the body, so that they might meet God profitably. **3.** For all the sons of blood shall be humbled [49] and ill-used, which are the sinners. And they shall look up to the height and fear shall be in the way [50]. This is the time when the soul of each one shall be plucked out in sorrow, where there is grief over evil works and rejoicing over good. **4.** Ought you not to fear God and his Christ Jesus and to tremble before him, we seeing the things

[Fragment 4] *ON REPENTANCE*

I. **1.** [be saved] from every evil and shelter them, strengthen them in their constancy, give power to them, and establish them that they may be saved from the snares of the devil and his plots, and from one who speaks nothing of truth, which is Satan [1]. **2.** And all men from whom you will get no gain in this place, you will pursue with your whirlwind and vex with your wrath and a fire shall devour them. The angel of the covenant shall take them and remove them outside the wall of the community, and shall moreover disperse them, even as the dust which the wind scatters upon the face of the earth, as it is written, 'Forasmuch as they loved the curse, it came upon them; they did not desire the blessing, it fled from them' [2].

II. **1.** * But let us, brethren, depart from the things which God and * p. 10
his Christ hate, and let us love the good, and also keep the commandments of our fathers, like the sons of Jonadab who kept the commandments of their father, over whom God watched and whom he saved from the wrath which came upon the people [3]. **2.** Thus it is with us : if we obey the words of our father and his teachings which he commanded us, the Lord will deliver us from every evil thing [4], as it has been said, 'My son, if you receive the words of my commandments and hide them with you, your ear will hear wisdom and you will pay heed to understanding [5]. Good counsel shall guard you and holy thought keep you [6], and strengthen

49 Cf. Eccles. 12. 4. — The reading 'blood' may have arisen from a confusion between the LXX reading *ᾄσματος*, and *αἵματος*, cf. W. H. Worrell, *Coptic Texts in the University of Michigan Collection*, Ann Arbor, 1942, p. 35. 50 Eccles. 12. 5.

1 Cf. Jn. 8. 44. 2 Cf. Ps. 108. 17. 3 Cf. Jer. 42. 6 ff. 4 Cf. II Tim. 4. 18. 5 Prov. 2. 1-2. 6 Prov. 2. 11.

your feet that you be not moved'[7]. **3.** Nevertheless, because of the multitude of my lawlessnesses, I shall bend my head and groan. I am shaken in all my members[8].

III. **1.** Woe to me, because my soul has failed before the murderers[9]. **2.** Woe to me, my mother, as what have you brought me forth? A man judged and set apart in the whole earth. I did not give profit, no one gave profit to me. My strength has failed among those who curse me[10]. **3.** Woe to me, because I have become like him who gathers stubble in the [harvest], and like him who collects [grapes of gleaning] in the vintage, when there is no bunch of grapes. Woe to me, because the godfearing has perished from the earth and the upright among men is not[11]. **4.** For no man is repenting of his wickedness saying, 'What have I done?' The runner has ceased from his course[12], while we did not say in our heart, 'Woe to us for we have sinned! That is why our heart was grieved'[13]. **5.** And we did not say, 'Let us then fear the Lord, our God[14], that we may turn away from our iniquities[15], and know in all truth'. Or, 'Come, let us weep before the Lord our maker'[16]. And, 'Come, let us worship and bow down to him[17], because he has made us and not we[18]. We are his people and the sheep of his hand'[19]. **6.** Or, 'Let us rend
* p. 11 our hearts and not our garments * and turn to the Lord our God[20] with fasting, weeping, and mourning[21], that he may abundantly forgive our sins'. **7.** For whenever we turn and sigh, then are we sober and know whence we are, lest we say we are alive while we are dead[22], lest we are dark while saying we are light.

IV. **1.** Forgive me; I entreat you all, brethren, that we should depart from these contemptible things and such great impieties which are disgraceful[23] to mention[24]. **2.** Do not let us be disdainful, do not let us be without fear. Remember that it has been said, 'He who does not fear shall be in places which the Eternal One does not visit'[25]. **3.** Remember us, for our span of life has ended in sorrow, ours and yours, and our years in sighings[26].

4[27]

[7] Prov. 3. 26. [8] Job 9. 27-28. [9] Jer. 4. 31. [10] Jer. 15. 10. [11] Cf. Mic. 7. 1-2. [12] Jer. 8. 6. [13] Lam. 5. 16-17. [14] Jer. 5. 24. [15] Cf. Jer. 5. 25. [16] Ps. 94. 6 b. [17] Ps. 94. 6 a. [18] Ps. 99. 3. [19] Ps. 94. 7. [20] Cf. Joel 2. 13. [21] Cf. Joel 2. 12. [22] Zoega CCIV reads: 'lest we are dead while saying we are alive'. [23] Zoega CCIV reads: 'shameful'. [24] Cf. Eph. 5. 12. [25] Prov. 19. 20. [26] Cf. Ps. 30. 11. [27] Zoega CCIV omits this number.

[Fragment 5] *ON FAITH, REPENTANCE, AND VIGILANCE*

5 [1]

I. **1.** 'Remember the Lord and let Jerusalem come into our [2] mind' [3], as it is written. And, 'Think of the Lord and you shall perform all my desires' [4]. **2.** For if man remembers the Lord and Jerusalem of heaven comes into his mind, no unclean thought nor any wickedness shall prevail over him, because he has built his house upon the rock [5] which is Christ [6], the hope of every man who sets his hope upon him, as it is written, 'I have put my trust in you, Lord, let me never be ashamed. Deliver me and save me in your righteousness. Incline * your ear to me and hasten to save me. * p. 12 Be to me a God of strength and a house of refuge to save me, for you are my defence and my refuge. For your name's sake, you will lead me and nurture me. You will bring me out of this snare which they have hidden for me, for you are my protector. I will commend my spirit into your hands, you have redeemed me, Lord God of truth. **3.** You have hated those who cherish vanities to no purpose, but I have trusted in the Lord. I will rejoice and be glad in your mercy, for you have regarded my humility and you have saved my soul from my afflictions. You have not given me into the hand of the enemy. You have set my feet in a spacious place [7]. For the angel of the Lord surrounds those who fear him and delivers them' [8].

II. **1.** So therefore, brethren, it is good for us to cleave to God and to put our hope on the Lord Christ, the Saviour of everyone who sincerely cries to him and who puts his trust in his mercy, that we may have help on the day of our tribulation and find mercy before him in the time of our affliction, which is the day of each one's visitation. **2.** For as it has been said, 'Possessions shall not profit on the day of wrath' [9], so also no wickedness, nor hatred, nor pride, nor quarrellers, murmurers, slanderers, whisperers, and no sinners of any kind who provoke God to anger, shall profit on the day of wrath, which is the day when the soul of each one shall be plucked out miserably, with no one to wipe the tears from our

1 Zoega CCIV omits this number. 2 Zoega CCIV reads : 'your'. 3 Jer. 28. 50. 4 Is. 44. 28. 5 Cf. Mt. 7. 24. 6 Zoega CCIV adds : 'who is'. 7 Ps. 30. 2-9. 8 Ps. 33. 8. 9 Prov. 11. 4.

eyes [10] and no one to hear us when we cry out. **3.** Instead we shall say, groaning in great wretchedness and weeping, 'Why did I not want them to teach me, and my heart turn away from reproofs [11], and did not incline my ear to him who instructs me?' [12] **4.** In like manner did the rich man, demented and groaning, ask for a drop of water in the burning of the fire which is in hell, and it was not
* p. 13 given to him, but other reproaches * and sorrows were told to him, as it is written in the gospel [13].

III. **1.** Let us therefore, brethren, strive, and let us depart from our wickednesses, our disobediences, our stiff-neckedness, our boastings, and turn and repent while there is time, before the day of our end comes upon us suddenly like a snare [14], and all these sufferings befall us, with no one to deliver us and no one to help us. **2.** Rather shall it be said to us rightly with reproach and contumely, 'When I called you, you did not hear me. And I spread abroad my words : you paid no heed. But you rejected my counsels and you disobeyed my upbraidings. **3.** I will also mock at your perdition and I will deride you when perdition comes upon you [15], and when tribulation comes to you and you are in straits [16] and trouble befalls you suddenly' [17], and the other words which come after these with which the sinners will be reproached and censured. **4.** Such will die in their sins not having regretted so as to turn and repent before they come into all these tribulations, as it is written, 'Salvation is far from the sinners because they did not seek after your statutes' [18].

IV. **1.** Therefore, brethren, let us be sober and vigilant [19], and labour at the work of the Lord always, that we may acquire for ourselves boldness before God in good works, for it has been said, 'The end of all is nigh. Be prudent, therefore, and be sober unto prayers' [20]. **2.** We remember the word which the Lord spoke, 'Let your loins be girded, your lamps burning, and be you like these men who look out for their lord, when he will return from the

[10] Cf. perhaps Rev. 7. 17. [11] Prov. 5. 12. [12] Prov. 5. 13. [13] Cf. Lk. 16. 19 ff. [14] Cf. Lk. 21. 34. [15] Prov. 1. 24-26. [16] Prov. 1. 27 b. — The noun **ⲕⲧⲟ** literally means : 'turning', 'return', 'what surrounds'. **ⲕⲧⲟ** here stands for *πολιορκία* in the LXX, which suggests the meaning 'besieging' hence 'to be in straits'. [17] Prov. 1. 27 a. [18] Ps. 118. 155. [19] Cf. I Thes. 5. 6, I Pet. 5. 8. [20] I Pet. 4. 7.

marriage; that if he come and knock, they shall open to him at once' [21], **3.** in order that we ourselves may become worthy for him to speak of us thus, 'Blessed are those servants whom their lord on coming finds vigilant. Verily, I say to you that he will gird himself and make them recline, and come forth and minister to them. * And if he should come in the second watch or the third and find them doing thus, blessed are those servants' [22]. * p. 14

V. **1.** O these great glorious wonders for those who shall become worthy of them! The Lord shall minister unto servants, God shall serve men. **2.** O blessed are the men who keep themselves from every wickedness and guard their heart and their body from every defilement and hate the evil and love the good [23]. For there are great good things laid up for them to inherit, as it is written, 'The things which eye saw not and ear heard not and which entered not into the heart of man, has God prepared for those who love him' [24]. **3.** Hear again that it has been said, 'Those who love God, for those who love God [25], are not contemptuous in anything, nor do they do what is unfitting' [26]. **4.** How great is the contentment and the joy and the gladness which shall be for those who shall be worthy of these things! It suffices only for them to see the Lord sitting on the throne of his glory [27] and calling them gladly, 'Come you blessed of my Father, and inherit the kingdom which was prepared [28]

[Fragment 6] *ON STRIFE IN THE COMMUNITY*

I. **1.** to do good [1]. And it has also been said, 'Lay hold on the good, abstain from every evil thing' [2]. **2.** But we, in our disobedience and the hardness of our unrepentant heart, have turned judgement into gall and the fruit of righteousness into bitterness [3], having laid hold on every evil and lawlessness. **3.** We have forsaken the good, and the peace, and the love of God, for judgement upon us and condemnation, drawing down upon ourselves a peril, as it is written, 'As they did not think fit to have God in their knowledge,

21 Lk. 12. 35-36. 22 Lk. 12. 37-38. 23 Cf. Amos 5. 15. 24 I Cor. 2. 9.
25 The repetition is probably an error. 26 I cannot identify this quotation.
27 Cf. Mt. 19. 28, Mt. 25. 31. 28 Mt. 25. 34.

1 Cf. perhaps Is. 1. 17. 2 I Thes. 5. 21-22. 3 Cf. Amos 6. 12.

God gave them over to a reprobate mind to do those things which are unseemly' [4], **4.** and the other words which come after these to * p. 15 which God has committed you, * you hard of heart because of your disobedience and your hatred of peace, since there is bitter envy in your heart, as it is written, 'Hatred raises strife' [5]. And as our father has said, '(To be) quarrellers is an attribute of the inhuman who are perverse'.

II. **1.** Why does fighting and trouble run before them like a fire wherever they go in the community, as it is written, 'A perverse man spreads strife and kindles the flame of deceit with evils and divides brethren and friends'? [6] **2.** Concerning these it has also been said, 'Evil men burn a city [7] and a community with their fighting and their strife and their bond of deceit'. 'For hatred raises strife' [8], as it is written. And again, 'Where jealousy and strife are, there is trouble and every evil deed' [9]. **3.** For if jealousy and hatred had not dominated your darkened heart, O pestilent men and unclean children who have forgotten their former sins [10], would you have rushed at one another and struck one another brazenly, being unafraid of the curse which our father spoke concerning this matter, 'Cursed is he who shall actually raise his hand against his neighbour with anything or with his hands in a blow [11] (either) without the elder or senselessly'? **4.** Or would you have cursed one another with disgraceful words shameful to utter [12], or would anyone really have listened to them, though no godfearing man in the world would say them, least of all a monk, except men who too are evil like you?

III. **1.** O wretched men who have not departed from their iniquities, nor yet feared the curse which our father spoke concerning these things also, 'Cursed is he who shall be at all contemptuous of his neighbour with any wicked word, in anger or in sport'. **2.** More especially the apostle commands, 'Let not a shameful word come out of your mouth [13], nor foolish talk, nor jesting, which are not fitting' [14]. **3.** To what word have we paid * p. 16 heed, or * wherein have we feared the Lord that we should rather

[4] Rom. 1. 28. [5] Prov. 10. 12. [6] Cf. Prov. 16. 28. [7] Prov. 29. 8. [8] Prov. 10. 12. [9] Cf. Jam. 3. 16. [10] Cf. II Pet. 1. 9. [11] Meaning doubtful, cf. W. E. Crum, *A Coptic Dictionary*, Oxford, 1939, p. 431 b. [12] Cf. perhaps Col. 3. 8, Eph. 5. 12. [13] Col. 3. 8. [14] Eph. 5. 4.

pay heed to these others? You do not listen to the Lord who says, 'He who shall be angry with his brother without cause is in danger of the judgement. He too who shall say to his brother, Division[15], is in danger of the council. And he who shall say, Fool, is in danger of the Gehenna of fire'[16]. **4.** Moreover he says, 'Every idle word that men shall speak, they shall give account thereof in the day of judgement'[17].

IV. **1.** Then whither shall wretches like us go, since we were not afraid to utter great vauntings from our mouth unrestrainedly, so that God had no satisfaction amongst us, as it is written, ' "My good pleasure was not upon you", says the Lord, your God. "For of old you broke your yoke and burst your bonds. You said, I will not be a servant" '[18]. **2.** This is your way too, for you break the fetters of our fathers from off you, and you cast their yoke of salvation away from you, which are their commandments which they have enjoined on us, in that you transgress them with great audacity, striking your neighbours without restraint and without fear of God, until God curses those who do these things and delivers them up to their own devices, even as it has been said, 'Whom I delivered unto Satan that he should teach them not to blaspheme'[19].

V. **1.** On this it has also been said, 'All evil men raise disputes, but God will send to them a merciless angel'[20], to punish them with strife, and quarrelling, and every evil thing. For strife and enmity shall not depart from such people, but shall seem death to them. **2.** For thus it has been said, 'Call them rejected silver, for the Lord has rejected them[21], and he has forsaken the generation which does these things'[22]. **3.** In all these things, moreover, their hearts do not blame them nor do they repent of what happened, as it is written, 'In all these things foolish Judah did not turn to me with all her heart, but to falsehood'[23], and they also walk in pride and ...

2 folios missing ...

15 ῥακά, which is in the Greek N.T., was apparently misunderstood and translated as if ῥαγάς, cf. CRUM, *Dictionary*, p. 281 a. 16 Mt. 5. 22. 17 Mt. 12. 36. 18 Jer. 2. 19-20. 19 I Tim. 1. 20. 20 Prov. 17. 11. 21 Jer. 6. 30. 22 Jer. 7. 29. 23 Jer. 3. 10.

[Fragment 7] *ON ESCHEWING EVIL*

* p. 17 I. **1.** * love towards one another and our peace, as it is written, 'Let them see your good works and glorify your Father which is in heaven'[1]. And again it is said, 'In this everyone shall know that you are my disciples, if you love each other'[2]. **2.** But if it is said, 'If you offer to me a blind beast for sacrifice, it is not good. And if you offer the lame or sick, it is not good'[3], and, 'Take it to your governor, will he accept it from you? Indeed if so, will he receive you?'[4] — then how shall God accept from us our prayers and our fasting and our recitation and the rest of our righteous deeds, if we defile our hearts and bodies with every foulness and every sin, or if we are disobedient, or if we lie to one another, or are full of envy and hatred towards one another, and quarrelling, pride, wickedness, evil, whispering, evil-speaking, boastfulness, and every bad thing. 'For those who do these things shall be fettered in their thoughts'[5], as it is written. **3.** But again it has been said, 'A son honours his father, and a servant fears his lord'[6]. But now it has been said, upbraiding our shamelessness and our impudence, ' "If then I am a father, where is my honour? And if I am a lord, where is my fear", says the Lord, the Almighty'[7].

II. **1.** But as for us, brethren, let us examine ourselves and fear God and honour him in good works and prepare ourselves to follow the Lord, our God, and seek the good and not the evil that we may live[8]. And let us eschew the things wherewith we provoke God to anger, which are our evil words which we speak against each other in our hard-heartedness. For if we despise our brother, we despise God who made us, since man was made in the image of God[9]. **2.** Therefore it is said, 'God is a spirit'[10]. Look to yourselves in your spirit, and eschew in your speech the things by which we provoke God to anger, lest he say to us in anger and contempt, * p. 18 ' "You who despise * my name, if you do not lay it to your heart to give glory to my name", says the Lord, the Almighty, "I will send the curse to you, and I will curse your blessing and scatter your

1 Cf. Mt. 5. 16. 2 Jn. 13. 35. 3 Cf. Mal. 1. 8. 4 Cf. Mal. 1. 8. 5 Cf. Prov. 20. 14. 6 Mal. 1. 6. 7 Mal. 1. 6. 8 Cf. Amos 5. 14. 9 Cf. Gen. 1. 26-27. 10 Cf. Jn. 4. 24.

blessing abroad, and it shall not be with you, because you do not lay it to your heart" '[11].

III. **1.** So then, brethren, let us turn and repent, because it has been said, 'If you do not turn, he will whet his sword and bend his bow and prepare it, having therewith prepared instruments of death'[12], **2.** so as to wipe out everyone who is wicked before him and destroy everyone who lies, everyone who hates his neighbour, everyone who walks in defilement, everyone who walks in thieving and lying, and everyone who is disobedient, who walks in stubbornness and pride, that he may wipe them out before him in the communities of God, according to what has been said, 'I will cast them out of my house, I will not love them any more[13], and I will destroy those who are disobedient'; **3.** lest it also be said to us threateningly, 'Is there not one God that created you? Is there not one father who is over you all? Why has each one of you forsaken his brother to defile the covenant of your fathers? Judah has dealt treacherously and has become an abomination in Israel and in Jerusalem'[14].

IV. **1.** But as for us, let us keep ourselves from defiling the covenant of our fathers, and let us not betray their teachings and their commandments, that we may not become an abomination before them. And let us not plot evil, each one against his brother[15], for it has been said, ' "All these things I hated", says the Lord'[16]. And, 'These things which I have hated, you have done'[17]. **2.** So then, brethren, let us depart from the things he hates, lest it be said to us sharply, 'Woe to them because they turned away from me; misery shall overtake them because they did iniquity against me'[18]. **3.** Or (lest) it be said to us in anger, 'The Lord destroys the man who does these things, until he is humbled into leaving the habitations of Jacob and from those who offer up sacrifice to the Lord, the Almighty'[19], * which are those who walk humbly and honourably without sin; according to that which has been said, 'And you shall turn and discern between a righteous and a lawless man, and between him who is a servant of God and him who is not a servant of God. **4.** For behold, the day of the Lord shall come, burning like a furnace,

* p. 19

11 Mal. 2. 2. 12 Ps. 7. 13-14. 13 Hos. 9. 15. 14 Mal. 2. 10-11. 15 Cf. Zech. 8. 17. 16 Zech. 8. 17. 17 Mal. 2. 13. 18 Hos. 7. 13. 19 Mal. 2. 12.

and consume them. And all the proud and all transgressors shall be like stubble and the day that is coming shall burn them [20]

[Fragment 8] *ON SINS OF THE TONGUE*

I. **1.** are his lips [1]. And, 'He who goads with words shall not be saved' [2]. And, 'An angry man prepares contentions' [3]. And, 'Wrath destroys even the wise' [4]. And, 'He who is quick to anger acts ill-advisedly' [5]. And, 'A grievous word raises wrath, but a word in its place turns away anger' [6]. **2.** We remember that which has been said, 'And this we know at this time that the hour has now come for us to arise from sleep [7]. The night is far spent, the day is at hand, let us therefore forsake the works of darkness' [8], which are provocations, evil-speakings [9], hatreds, and boastings, that we may live in propriety and in attendance upon the Lord honourably without anxiety [10], and in sinlessness.

II. **1.** But you who make these disturbances and who lie one to another, woe to you, for you have not remembered the word which our father said sorrowfully, 'Again you lie one to another in hatred after hearing the curse that he who lies to his neighbour in wickedness and hatred is cursed'. Or will you be able to vindicate the words which you [11] utter slanderously? **2.** If the things you say are true, woe to you because you did not say them at the time or the
* p. 20 occasion when it was suitable to say them. For * to speak a word in its season is altogether good [12]. **3.** But if the things you say are lies, woe to you. You shall be greatly cursed because you have lied [13] to your brethren and you have thought out schemes which you will not be able to vindicate, drawing down upon yourselves wrath in the day of wrath and the revelation of the just judgement of God, who will render to every man according to his works [14]. **4.** For on this

20 Mal. 3. 18-4. 1.

1 Cf. perhaps Prov. 18. 7. 2 Prov. 19. 4. 3 Prov. 15. 18. 4 Prov. 15. 1. 5 Prov. 14. 17. 6 Cf. Prov. 15.1. 7 Rom. 13. 11. 8 Rom. 13. 12. 9 Cf. II Cor. 12. 20. 10 Cf. I Cor. 7. 35. 11 The text : 'lies ... the words which you', fragmentary in Insinger 57, has been completed from K. 9224. 12 Cf. perhaps Prov. 15. 23 (especially the Hebrew text). 13 The text : 'woe to you ... lied', fragmentary in Insinger 57, has been completed from K. 9224. 14 Rom. 2. 5-6.

it has been said, ‘The lover of sin rejoices in contentions’[15]. And, ‘The hard of heart will meet with no good’[16].

[Fragment 9] *ON OBEDIENCE*

I. **1.** from every evil[1]. Let us obey him who urges us and encourages us towards the teaching which says, ‘My son, if you receive the words of my commandment and hide them with you, your ear will hear wisdom and you will pay heed to understanding and give it to your son as teaching’[2]. **2.** And again, ‘My son, do not be lax, keep my counsel and my opinion that your soul may live and that grace may be about your neck. Then there shall be healing for your flesh and care for your bones, that you may walk confidently in peace on all your ways and that your foot may not stumble’[3]. **3.** And again, ‘Keep my commandments and do not forget them, and do not forget the word of my mouth. Do not forsake it and it shall receive you unto itself; love it and it shall guard you[4]. Turn it to yourself and it shall exalt you; honour it in order that it may receive you unto itself, that it may put a crown of grace upon your head and protect you with a crown of delight’[5]. **4.** Therefore, do not let us be negligent, lest we repent at our end and say sorrowfully, ‘Why did I not want them to teach me, and my heart turn away from reproofs?’[6] or say, * ‘I did not listen to the voice of him * p. 21 who teaches me, and did not incline my ear to him who instructs me’[7]. **5.** And do not let us forget the commandments which have been given to us, lest we are scolded with disgrace, ‘When I called you, you did not hear me. And I spread abroad my words : you paid no heed. But you rejected my counsels and you disobeyed[8] ...

1 folio missing ...

[Fragment 10] *ON OBEDIENCE*

I. **1.** because they saw you being subject to those who are greater than yourselves according to that which the apostle has said, ‘Imitate

15 Prov. 17. 19. 16 Prov. 17. 20.

1 Cf. perhaps Prov. 1. 33. 2 Prov. 2. 1-2. 3 Prov. 3. 21-23. 4 Prov. 4. 4-6. 5 Prov. 4. 8-9. 6 Prov. 5. 12. 7 Prov. 5. 13. 8 Prov. 1. 24-25.

me even as I have imitated Christ' [1]. **2.** For it has also been said [2], 'Those who imitate Christ, imitate vigorously; and those who have put on Christ [3] vigorously, make Christ take form in them [4] in all their life, in frame of mind, in speech, in behaviour, in deeds, in constancy, in love perfect towards God'. **3.** And you, brethren, obey your fathers who [teach] you [according to] God, in all [obedience], in fear and trembling, in singleness of your heart [5] as [being subject] to the [Lord, not man], knowing that the good which each man and each woman shall do he shall receive from the Lord Jesus [6], whether father, or son, or mother, or daughter. **4.** The apostle also says, 'But we beseech you, brethren, to know [those that labour] among [you] and preside over you in the Lord and [teach] you, and to esteem them [highly in love because of their work]' [7]. **5.** Therefore, be vigilant, do not let us hear that any woman of you or any man of us has disobeyed those who teach you, that our heart be saddened,
* p. 22 and you grieve yourselves and we * too be grievously saddened. As the apostle has said, 'Lest by any means I should come to you and find you not as I wish, and you should find me [not] as you wish me' [8].

[Fragment 11] *TO AN ERRING MONK*

I. **1.** into the houses and communities without asking and without an order. You walk in the darkness of your disobedience which is in the corruption and the wickedness of your evil-begetting heart. You walk in a way fraught with peril and readily accursed. **2.** O blind brother, whose soul nourishes his heart with passions and fleshly lusts, you are ignorant (of the fact) that you are despising the grace of God and bringing shame on those that have (it) not with your recklessness and your self-will [1]. **3.** For the place of which you said, 'I am going there', is one thing, while the

1 I Cor. 11. 1. 2 For the following quotation, cf. I Pseudo-Clementine De Virginitate, VII, see L. Th. Lefort, 'Une citation copte de la Ia Pseudo-clémentine "De virginitate" ', *Bulletin de l'Institut français d'archéologie orientale*, 30, pp. 509 ff.; see also L. Th. Lefort, *Les Pères Apostoliques en copte*, Louvain, 1952, CSCO, 135/Copt.17, p. 40, and 136/*Copt.18*, p. 34. 3 Cf. Gal. 3. 27, Rom. 13. 14. 4 Cf. Gal. 4. 19. 5 Cf. Eph. 6. 5. 6 Cf. Eph. 6. 7-8. 7 I Thes. 5. 12-13. 8 II Cor. 12. 20.

1 Cf. II Pet. 2. 10.

place to which you went is another, because you are a bloody man. 'For bloody and deceitful men shall not remember the days of their end' [2], as it is written. **4.** You draw down the curse of God upon you and the destruction of your soul, since you have not that which guides you, namely the commandment of God, as it is written, 'Those without guidance fall like leaves' [3].

II. **1.** You, indeed, are darkness with its evil works and not a brother of light. You did not know nor did you learn wisdom, walking in the dark and saying in your pestilent heart, 'Who has seen me, and who shall know concerning me of the things which I do stealthily?' [4] **2.** You did not remember that which is written, 'Woe to those who take secret counsel which is not from the Lord. Woe to those who take counsel stealthily and their works shall be in the dark' [5]. **3.** And, 'Woe to the rebellious children. You have taken counsel which is not from me and pledges not from my spirit to add sin upon sin' [6]. **4.** You do not understand that as it was in the case of your father Judas, who fell upon his face, burst asunder * and all his bowels gushed out [7], so it is in your case, God * p. 23
and his Christ having revealed the wickednesses which you have perpetrated, which no man knows, because your works are his. **5.** That man is a thief and a sinner in everything, a stealer of that which is cast into the bag [8]. So also are you, taking the loaves of offering, giving them to whomsoever you wish to give, covertly, without restraint and without asking. **6.** You did not consider and you did not reflect that it is a fearful thing to come into the hands of the living God [9]. **7.** Moreover you did not remember that it is a fearful thing to expect the judgement and the fierceness [10] of the fire which will devour the adversaries [11]. Who are the adversaries of whom mention is made except those who do evil and transgress the commandment like you and all those who resemble you, in the way in which you did not reflect before going into a town, or house, or strange community? **8.** You spent the whole night outside without any man knowing. You draw down upon yourself

[2] Cf. Ps. 54. 24. — The LXX, following the Hebrew, reads : *οὐ μὴ ἡμισεύσωσι τὰς ἡμέρας αὐτῶν*. For a Greek reading supporting the Sah., cf. A. Rahlfs, *Septuaginta-Studien*, Göttingen, 1904 ff., Heft 2, p. 157. [3] Prov. 11. 14. [4] Cf. Is. 29. 15. [5] Is. 29. 15. [6] Is. 30. 1. [7] Acts 1. 18. [8] Cf. Jn. 12. 6. [9] Heb. 10. 31. [10] Cf. p. 8, n. 35. [11] Heb. 10. 27.

the wrath of God unwittingly. **9.** If no man knows the things which you do covertly or which you do in the darkness, does God not know either? Do you not hear, '"Shall anyone be able to hide himself in a secret place and I not see him? Do I not fill the heaven and the earth?" says the Lord'? [12]

III. **1.** Therefore, wicked son, woe to you, because not only were you not content with your impieties, but you also deceived a youth, dragging him along with you into your sins, because the snare of the hunter, that is to say the devil, is upon all your ways [13], as when a blind man is leading a blind man and both fall into a pit [14]. **2.** If you had really been in awe and had taken heed of the saying of your fathers, you would not have ventured upon such recklessnesses. Do you not hear, 'The foolish and the ignorant shall perish together'? [15] **3.** On those who become dark, the foxes shall feed [16], which means that in those who transgress the commandments will the devil and his demons feed. For if the eyes of your mind had not been closed and the senses of your soul destroyed, you would not have attempted these great acts of irreverence. **4.** Do you not know that him who destroys the wall, * p. 24 the serpent will bite [17], which is the devil. Or * has it not again been said, 'He who keeps the commandment is saved' [18]. **5.** And also, 'He who keeps the commandment shall know no evil thing [19]. For indeed, the son who forsakes instruction will cherish evils and will meditate iniquitous words [20]. And the son who is perverse in receiving teaching shall fall into evils' [21]. And also, 'The evil son is haughty [22] and his teeth are knives' [23]. And, 'The iniquitous son judges himself to be righteous but he has not purified his way' [24]. **6.** For thus it has also been said, 'Everyone who does not learn to do righteousness in the land will not act honestly' [25]. On this it has also been said, 'Woe unto them who call evil good and good evil, who count darkness for light and light for darkness, who say that bitter is sweet and sweet is bitter. Woe unto them that are wise in their own eyes and prudent in their own sight' [26].

12 Jer. 23. 24. 13 Cf. Hos. 9. 8. 14 Cf. Mt. 15. 14. 15 Ps. 48. 11. 16 Cf. perhaps Lam. 5. 18. 17 Eccles. 10. 8. 18 Cf. Prov. 13. 13. 19 Eccles. 8. 5. 20 Prov. 19. 24. 21 Cf. Prov. 17. 16. 22 Prov. 24. 36. 23 Prov. 24. 37. 24 Prov. 24. 35. 25 Is. 26. 10. 26 Is. 5. 20-21.

IV. **1.** Therefore, rebellious son, if your ignorant heart had not become dark, or if you had not counted darkness for light and light for darkness, or if bitter had not been sweet in your opinion and sweet bitter, would you have been so greatly daring as to go whither you were not sent, or would you have gone out from here without asking? **2.** And if your heart had not been as leprous as Gehazi's, the deceitful son, who went out stealthily from the prophet Elisha and made the man turn back and received from him money and put it into a dark place like his works which were also dark; especially as he was also lying when, having been asked, 'Where did you go?' he said, 'Your servant went nowhere', until he was told of his rebellion, 'Was not my heart going along with you when you made the man turn back from the chariot to receive from him gold and silver that his leprosy might cleave to you and your seed for ever'[27]. **3.** So also is your case, when you were asked, 'From where are you coming?' you lied, 'I did not go anywhere'. You too did not know that the eyes of God look in every place upon the wicked and the good[28]. In particular he also looks at you the more as you walk in the way of your lawlessness and your disobedience and the hardness of your heart which is distressing and full of leprosy. **4.** And you did not remember that which is written, * 'Because of your hardness and your impenitent heart you treasure up for yourself wrath in the day of wrath and the revelation of the just judgement of God, who will render to every man according to his works'[29]. * p. 25

V. **1.** In the place to which you went, they do not mock you thus and despise you, unless their heart is unlike yours. They still also blaspheme the name of God and despise the name of our fathers after it had already been told us, 'On no account, then, let the name of God be blasphemed because of us'[30], and the name of our father be despised because of our ignorance. **2.** But the name of God is blessed and holy, and the name of our fathers is honoured and holy, but our faces will burn with ignominy and we shall be put to shame. **3.** Our fathers are innocent of our blood and our condemnation which shall come upon us, for they did their

27 Cf. IV Kg. 5. 21 ff. 28 Prov. 15. 3. 29 Rom. 2. 5-6. 30 Cf. Is. 52. 5, Rom. 2. 24, I Tim. 6. 1.

utmost for us in every respect. And they told us at the outset in their teaching not to fall into evil, as it is written, 'He who does not tell his son at the outset to guard himself from evil will perish suddenly'[31]. **4.** But we, in our impudence, our shamelessness, and our senselessness, have not paid heed to their words of light which they enjoined upon us, until we have come into all these evils. **5.** Therefore I promise you : if you do not examine yourself and speak the truth and confess what you have done and turn and sigh and rend your heart and not your garments[32], the wrath of God will proceed to work upon you strangely[33]. **6.** Even so lawlessness has corrupted you and stunned you, as it is written, 'Transgressions ensnare the ignorant man and they bind everyone fast in the bonds of his sins'[34], until God hates you and casts you out of his house, as it has been said, 'I will cast them out of my house, I will not love them any more'[35]. **7.** And it is also said, 'God shall cast them out from him because they did not listen to him, and they shall be wanderers among the nations'[36].

* p. 26 VI. **1.** Therefore take yourself off — (all of) you bloody * and deceitful men and transgressors, from the holy places of God[37], because your way is not pleasant before him. **2.** For the wicked shall not stay with him, nor shall the transgressors continue before his eyes. For the Lord has hated everyone who works lawlessness and he will destroy everyone who lies[38]. **3.** Therefore, brethren, all of us together, whether great or small, whether man or woman, do not let us pay heed to those who are ignorant time after time among us and those who walk after their hearts' desire, but let us strive, remembering that which has been said[39], 'To those who are disobedient time after time no right thing happens, but they endure months of vanity[40] in this world'. **4.** Moreover the apostle says, 'If in this life only we believe in Christ, then we are more miserable than all men'[41]. **5.** (Let us strive) lest also our fathers go to law with us as it was said that Elijah is still now going to law with us when he says, 'How long, Israel, will you limp on both feet? Either

31 Prov. 24. 22. — This clause, though in the Sah. (W. H. Worrell, *The Proverbs of Solomon in Sahidic Coptic*, Chicago, 1931), is not in the LXX.
32 Cf. Joel 2. 13. 33 Cf. Is. 28. 21. 34 Prov. 5. 22. 35 Hos. 9. 15.
36 Hos. 9. 17. 37 Cf. Ps. 5. 7-8. 38 Cf. Ps. 5. 5-7. 39 For the following quotation, cf. p. 74. 40 Cf. Job 7. 3. 41 I Cor. 15. 19.

God is God, or Baal is Baal' [42]. **6.** If then the commandments of our fathers are established with us, let us walk in them honourably and sinlessly. If also our aspiration is honourable before us, then let us go to the place where we shall find freely our aspiration. For this place is the house of God and the vineyard of the saints. **7.** (Let us strive) lest also the word which is written says to us according to our deserts, 'For it is not a people with understanding; therefore he that made them will not have pity upon them and he who formed them will not have mercy on them' [43].

VII. **1.** But let us listen to that which is said, 'Learn to do righteousness, inhabitants of the earth. For the ungodly has perished' [44]. **2.** And let us be worthy to say, 'Lord God, grant us peace, for you have repaid all to us according to our works. Lord our God, keep us with you. Lord, we know no other beside you, we proclaim your name. But those who are dead in sin shall not see life, and the physicians shall not rise' [45]. **3.** These are they concerning whom it has been said, 'But you are unrighteous physicians * and * p. 27 healers of all those who are evil' [46]. Moreover, these are they who corrupt hearts and who beguile the hearts of the innocent [47] and who walk in disaffection and babblings and unfounded talk, being vainly exalted by their fleshly mind [48], who are not at all suitable to be men of God, and especially not monks. **4.** For if we had remembered how we shall meet God and how we shall stand at the judgement-seat of Christ and each one receive according to his works [49], we would not have quarrelled arrogantly in boldness with those appointed to take care of us, nor would we have fought with our brethren in hatred, nor would we have thought up evil against one another. **5.** Or if we had remembered how we shall be punished in hell, we would not have planned wickedness against our neighbour in hardness of heart and hatred, nor would we have defiled our bodies, nor would we have corrupted each other's heart, weakly acting as a drag on them. Thus we are going to and fro in the imagination of our evil hearts and malicious madness [50].

VIII. **1.** So then, brethren, let us depart from these instabilities,

[42] Cf. III Kg. 18. 21. [43] Is. 27. 11. [44] Is. 26. 9-10. [45] Is. 26. 12-14. [46] Job 13. 4. [47] Cf. Rom. 16. 18. [48] Cf. Col. 2. 18. [49] Cf. II. Cor. 5. 10. [50] Cf. Eccles. 10. 13.

for we shall be past repentance and break our hearts when there is no one to hear us. **2.** For there is yet a little while, yet a little while, await tribulation upon tribulation. And there is yet a little while, yet a little while, await hope upon hope [51]. **3.** Or shall we run to that which runs to us, brethren? Indeed, we shall strive painfully with all our might until we escape. If you have strength to endure punishments and an unquenchable fire and a worm that never dies [52], you know it. We have not the strength. **4.** Then God and our Lord Jesus, the Merciful One, full of compassion, shall take pity on our misery and our wretchedness, and shall have mercy on our poverty and our weakness. For who else is God except he who takes away the lawlessnesses and overlooks the iniquities of
* p. 28 the remnant of his inheritance [53]. **5.** Therefore, as * it has been said, 'Come, let us bow down and worship him and weep before the Lord our maker, because he is our God and we are his people and the sheep of his hand [54]. For we are his creation, he having redeemed us [55] in Christ Jesus for good works, which God has prepared before in order that we should walk in them' [56].

IX. **1.** Now, brethren, let us depart from these pointless contentions, quarrels, and hatreds, for they are without profit and vain, lest it be said to us also, 'Whence are these wars and these fightings which are among you? Are they not from your pleasures that war in your members? You lust and you have not [57]; you fight and war; you have not because you ask not. You ask and receive not because you ask wrongly, that you may spend in your pleasures' [58] : **2.** lest also it be said to us after we have been taught, 'Lord, your eyes look upon faith; you scourged them and they were not grieved; you destroyed them and they did not want to receive instruction. They made their faces harder than a rock, and they did not want to return. **3.** But I said, "Perhaps they are poor, because they were not strong, for they did not know the way of the Lord and the judgement of God. But I shall go to the strong and speak with them, because they knew the way of the Lord and the judgement of God". **4.** And, behold, together

[51] Cf. Is. 28. 10, Is. 28. 13. [52] Cf. Is. 66. 24, Mk. 9. 48. [53] Cf. Mic. 7. 18. [54] Ps. 94. 6-7. [55] Perhaps in error for : 'he having created us'. [56] Eph. 2. 10. [57] Jam. 4. 1-2. [58] Jam. 4. 2-3.

they have broken the yoke and burst the bonds. Therefore a lion out of the forest leapt at them[59] — which is the devil — and a wolf obliterated them up to their houses, and a leopard sat in ambush by their cities. They shall seize everyone who comes out of them, because they multiplied their iniquities, they waxed strong in their deviations'[60]. This also means the devil and Satan and his demons. **5.** Concerning him it has been said, 'He goes, roaring as the lions, seeking * to devour our wretched souls'[61], * p. 29 because we did not follow honourably after God so as to know the way of the Lord and the judgement of God.

X. **1.** Therefore it is also said, ' "The heaven was troubled about this matter and the earth trembled greatly", says the Lord, "because my people have done two evil things. They have forsaken me, the fountain of living water, they have dug for themselves broken cisterns which will not be able to hold water" '[62]. **2.** This means that we forsook the true teaching and followed our own teaching, which is our wicked desires, because we did not hold fast our good initial attitude, when we had entered, and our gratitude and humility, as it is written, 'For we have become partakers of Christ if we hold fast the beginning of the confidence firm unto the end'[63]. **3.** For on this it is said, blaming us when our heart changes and we turn towards evil, 'I planted you as a vine wholly bearing true fruit. How did you turn to bitterness, vine that became strange?'[64] **4.** It is also still said angrily, ' "Though you wash yourself in natron and multiply for yourself lye, you have been greatly defiled in iniquity before me", says the Lord'[65]. **5.** May it come to pass then that the Lord grant us that we may guard ourselves from evil and that we may keep his commandments and the teachings of our fathers, so that we may find grace and obtain mercy in time for us for a help[66].

[Fragment 12] *REPROOFS AND MONASTIC RULES*

Lord, I remembered you in tribulation, your teaching came to us in a little tribulation, and like her who is in travail and near to bringing forth, who cried out at her pain of travail, thus have we

[59] Jer. 5. 3-6. [60] Jer. 5. 6. [61] Cf. I Pet. 5. 8. [62] Jer. 2. 12-13.
[63] Heb. 3. 14. [64] Jer. 2. 21. [65] Jer. 2. 22. [66] Heb. 4. 16.

become your beloved. For fear of you, O Lord, we conceived, we were in travail, we brought forth. You have put a spirit of salvation upon the earth [1].

I. **1.** Many words, brethren, in many ways has our father spoken in great sorrow, either with grief and anger, or with entreaty and * p. 30 consolation, or with blessings and curses, * for he wishes us to escape the judgement of God and to be saved from the wrath which shall be revealed from heaven [1a], because we are his sons, and we are the creation of the hands of God. But we did not perceive and we did not take to ourselves his teachings so as to be saved. Therefore, woe to those who are disobedient amongst us, and who hate the good and love the evil [2]. **2.** Furthermore, thieves are found remaining amongst us. Moreover it is heard that they have been stealing clothes here, or shoes, and whatever they find they take, going and giving them to their relatives who have left these communities, or have been expelled from them because of their misdeeds. **3.** Some are found, too, secretly outside the wall talking to people related to them or unrelated to them, who have departed from amongst us, without asking, in the evening or at night, or in the morning. They were not afraid of the curse which is written concerning these deeds, nor did they revere the commandment.

II. **1.** O, the hope of those who perpetrate these deeds and who steal anything and anywhere is cursed, and they are the more spurned and rejected before God and his Christ. **2.** Wicked men, indeed, and sons of the devil, enemies of righteousness are they who pervert the upright by their perfidious deeds; and rebellious sons who bring shame on those that have (it) not and who despise the commandment of God. **3.** Therefore you are cursed the more. Where is the freedom which is in our monastery, these things being unknown to us before to-day? **4.** Even as those are cursed who shall steal anything anywhere in these communities, from a cord to a shoestrap [2a], more especially a garment and a cloak or a cowl and shoes or anything else at all, the more are those also cursed who shall give anything to a man, whether (he is) in the community or any other man outside among those who have departed from us. **5.** And the curses which our father has uttered in all his epistles

1 Is. 26. 16-18. 1a Cf. Rom. 1. 18. 2 Cf. Mic. 3. 2. 2a Gen. 14. 23.

and all which have been uttered in the scriptures shall come upon everyone who is deceitful and who steals among us, until he[3] blots them out together with all their sufferings so that they do not benefit by anything that they do. **6.** Deceitful and perverse sons, senseless ones, are these the things with which you will repay the Lord? This is the way of a foolish people * without wisdom. Will you * p. 31 not fear the Lord, or will you not be in awe before him?[4] **7.** For on this it has been said, 'The heart of this people was hardened and they were slow to hear with their ears, and they shut their eyes lest they might return and God forgive them'[5]. **8.** And also, 'But this people has got a disobedient and unbelieving heart : they turned away and departed; they did not say in their heart, "Let us then fear the Lord, our God" '[6], who made us worthy to be brought into this freedom which is unknown to us. **9.** Our disobedience will teach us, and our wickedness will upbraid us. Know and see that it is bitter for us to forsake the commandments of God[7] and our fathers.

III. **1.** Woe to us for we have sinned! That is why our heart was grieved[8]. What shall I say to you? Can it be that you are not ashamed? I am ashamed for you. Can it be that you are not afraid? There is a place where you shall break your hearts, for there will be no one who will hear you and no one who will wipe your tears from your eyes[9]. **2.** False brethren, indeed, and deceivers, insatiable thieves, sons of Judas the traitor[10], enemies of purity and truth! Those who do such things are not only cursed together with their works, but they are also cursed in their going in and their going out and their recitation and their prayer, as it is written, 'Let their prayer become sin unto them[11]. **3.** Forasmuch as they loved the curse, it came upon them; they did not desire the blessing, it fled from them. They put on the curse like a garment. It went like water into their bowels and like oil into their bones'[12]. **4.** The Lord destroys deceitful men who do these things until they are humbled into leaving his communities[13]. And he scatters them like twigs and stubble which the wind carries afar, because they

[3] I.e. God. [4] Cf. Jer. 5. 22. [5] Cf. Is. 6. 10, Mt. 13. 15. [6] Jer. 5. 23-24. [7] Cf. Jer. 2. 19. [8] Lam. 5. 16-17. [9] Cf. perhaps Rev. 7. 17. [10] Cf. Lk. 6. 16. [11] Cf. Ps. 108. 7. [12] Cf. Ps. 108. 17-18. [13] Cf. Mal. 2. 12.

have not remembered to act honestly. **5.** For even as it has been said, 'Thus shall the wave take the unrighteous'[14], so shall the wave and the fury of the wrath of God take every deceitful, godless one away from his holy monasteries, whether man or woman. **6.** And where are you going before him, or where will you hide yourselves so that he does not see you in your deceptions? Even * p. 32 so do you hide yourselves from men, * saying in your darkened heart, being in straits, 'Who shall see us? And who shall know concerning us of the things which we do?'[15] **7.** Shall not all who act lawlessly know, when they are afraid in the place where there is no fear[15a], concerning their deceptions and their wicked deeds, and shall they not recognise their iniquities? **8.** Therefore, you (must) settle it with God, for our father has gone to Christ saddened because of such deeds. Moreover he grieves over us now in the place where he is because of our irregular doings. **9.** Nevertheless, I shall say thus with much sighing and anguish : if he was not saying to us in anger and rage and wrath, 'Tell them, "Prepare yourselves, for, behold, the bridegroom is coming[16] to visit you, God and the Son of God" ', would he who hears be weeping, seeing how angry he is in great indignation, fearing lest he come and find us unprepared and say to one of us or to some amongst us, 'Friend or friends, how did you come hither, without wearing a wedding-garment?'[17]

IV. **1.** How great is the sorrow, and the grief, and the sighing, and the shame, which will overtake us at the time when we shall be separated from the brethren who are innocent and guiltless of every evil deed, who are of one mind with God and with our fathers, and who walk in simplicity of heart and integrity. In particular, it has been said to us in severity, 'Bind their hands and their feet, cast them out into the outer darkness'[18]. **2.** How great is the contentment of heart and the joy and the consolation which shall overtake the brethren who walk in purity, and truth, and obedience in all things, and righteousness, and humility, if the King, the Lord of glory, Jesus, the Son of God, come and say to them, 'Come you blessed of my Father, and inherit the kingdom which was

[14] Is. 57. 20. [15] Cf. Is. 29. 15. [15a] Cf. Ps. 13. 4-5. [16] Cf. Mt. 25. 6.
[17] Cf. Mt. 22. 12. [18] Cf. Mt. 22. 13.

prepared for you from the foundation of the world'[19]. I will hear your words to set you at ease because you have heard mine also. **3.** Or again, if he was not saying once more in this same sorrow and this same grief, 'How long am I to perform these deeds of a leader or a soldier?[20] Remove this * dry wood and these things and * p. 33 let them be cast[21] out of the midst of this place and cleanse it', would he who hears be grieved, seeing how angry he is, knowing of which defiled things he speaks?

V. **1.** Therefore, woe to those who take to themselves the works of the devil, who despise the works of God and forget his words and reject his commandments. **2.** Are not the works of the devil thefts, lies, pollutions, abominations, enmities, deceptions, estrangements, wastings of time, lustful embroiderings of garments, and washings of one's feet and face, desiring one's face to be beautified in the flesh? **3.** They remembered not the word which is written, 'Do not take care for your flesh concerning its lusts'[22]. For those who do these things shall be fettered in their evil thoughts[23]. **4.** For the thought of the flesh is enmity against God, for it is not subject to the law of God nor, indeed, can it be[24]. And they that are in the flesh, who do these evil deeds, will not be able to please God[25]. But the wrath of God will come upon them and they are cursed in their evil deeds which they perpetrate, which are disgraceful to mention[26]. **5.** And woe to them, because it has been said, 'My spirit shall not dwell in these men for ever, because they are flesh'[27]. For where the Spirit of the Lord is, there is freedom[28] from every evil deed. But where the spirit of the devil is, there is every wickedness. **6.** And those who do these things shall be bound in impure thoughts and shall not be able to escape because God has departed from them. They shall fall and shall not be able to rise[29]. For lawlessness has gained power over them. **7.** And God has cast them out from him because they have not obeyed him, even as it is written, ' "My good pleasure was not

19 Mt. 25. 34. 20 Cf. perhaps Zoega CLXXXVI, ⲥⲓⲁ̅, G. Zoega, *Catalogus codicum copticorum manuscriptorum*, Rome, 1810, p. 388. 21 Meaning doubtful, cf. Crum, *Dictionary*, p. 586 a. 22 Rom. 13. 14. 23 Cf. Prov. 20. 14. 24 Rom. 8. 7. 25 Cf. Rom. 8. 8. 26 Cf. Eph. 5. 12. 27 Gen. 6. 3. 28 II Cor. 3. 17. 29 Cf. Amos 5. 2.

upon you", says the Lord your God [30]. "For of old you burst your bonds. You said, I will not be a servant" ' [31].

VI. **1.** But you, brethren, who fear God and love purity and truth, blessed are you. The Lord will bless you and guard you * p. 34 from the evil one [32], and he will save * you into his kingdom which is in heaven [33]. **2.** Formerly, before to-day, we had not yet come into this way of life, and we had not yet known God so as to understand what is fitting. We were walking, everyone, after our hearts' desire, doing the desires of the flesh and our thoughts, being by nature children of wrath [34], as it is written, walking in defilements, thefts, lies, and lusts, without anyone to teach us and to rebuke us. **3.** But now we have known God and, what is more, God has known us. And we have been taught and instructed in his law and his commandments, and we have known death and life. **4.** We have also been told, 'Behold the blessing and the curse'. And we have been charged, 'Choose for yourselves the life', that is to say, how you may live [35], after we know the good and the evil. **5.** We still turn and are entangled in these perverse deeds which yield no profit but only loss, and we provoke the wrath of God against ourselves. These are defilements, abominations, thefts, lies, desires of our impure hearts, embroidering of garments, and improper washings, after we have been taught concerning all these things and ordered not to do them. But we are again entangled in them and fall [36].

VII. **1.** It will be said justly of us, 'It were better for you, had you not known the way of righteousness, rather than that, knowing it, you turn back from the holy commandment given to you' [37]. **2.** And they shall be cursed with all their works, and their constancy is to no purpose for them. For they endure months of great vanity [38] in this world, especially as they were told and did not listen. **3.** But they turned once more to the filth like swine, and like dogs which turn to their vomit [39]; and they are hated by God and by men, because they have forsaken the fear of God and have not remembered their end. **4.** So then we lay down this also,

[30] Jer. 2. 19. [31] Cf. Jer. 2. 20. [32] II Thes. 3. 3. [33] Cf. II Tim. 4. 18. [34] Eph. 2. 3. [35] Cf. Deut. 30. 19. [36] Cf. II Pet. 2. 20. [37] Cf. II Pet. 2. 21. [38] Cf. Job 7. 3. [39] Cf. II Pet. 2. 22, Prov. 26. 11.

considering that we desire that stability should be ours, and that we should benefit by what we do. I am referring to the craftsmen : every pair of shoes which they shall make and everything which they shall produce shall be given to the men appointed for them, in order that everything which was handed in to them shall be asked * for from them — either girdle, thong, or shoesole — that * p. 35 there may be contentment among you, one with another, and that there may be peace and love in your hearts for one another. **5.** For we are here for this, and this is the will of God and his Christ. For we do not take thought for hide or shoes only or any other such thing, but we rather take thought for our soul which the whole world is not worth [40], and we wish that the Lord Jesus may have mercy upon us and that we may find grace in his presence at the time of our need.

VIII. **1.** Not only these, but also all other crafts including the carpenters, and the smiths, and the potters [41]; or the sack-weavers, or the linen-weavers; including the basket-makers, and the tailors; and, above all, the scribes or the bookbinders — they shall not give even a farthing [42] to any man, either amongst us or outside, nor any product they make. **2.** Every article they produce they shall hand in to the men appointed for them, in order that they may know everything which is made. For they shall render account to God, and them shall the father of these communities question concerning every article. **3.** And no one in any craft shall give anything to anyone without the elder or without those who are appointed for them. He who gives anything to anyone on his own without having asked or without having been told — from a strap to a pair of shoes, or a girdle, or a pouch [43], or pincers to extract thorns, or a nail, or a sickle, or a spade [44], or a tool [45], or a peg, or a point of a tool [45] — on his own authority, including anything at all, or gives to them secretly, will be liable to the wrath of God which will come upon all sinners because they did not repent. **4.** So then, he who will go on doing this abomination yet

40 Cf. Mt. 16. 26, Mk. 8. 36, Heb. 11. 38. 41 Meaning doubtful, cf. ⲥⲉⲕⲱⲧ, CRUM, *Dictionary*, p. 123 a. 42 Lit. : 'carat'. 43 Meaning doubtful, cf. CRUM, *Dictionary*, p. 397 a. 44 Or : 'pick'. 45 Meaning doubtful, cf. CRUM, *Dictionary*, p. 103 b, and especially *Zeitschrift der deutschen morgenländischen Gesellschaft*, 68, p. 183.

again, that is to say that they embroider their garments, or wash themselves to excess improperly, or steal, or lie, or defile themselves in any way, shall be cursed with God and men, and every godfearing man shall say, 'It shall be so' [46]. **5.** Behold these things : thus have we spoken. He who will not desist after these things will, I think, not have contentment but each one shall have done to him according to his deserts.

* p. 36 IX. **1.** * No man shall go to the infirmary to visit anybody without having asked first, or without having been sent, in the morning, or at midday, or in the evening, especially after coming out from eating, or at night. He who will be found there at those times shall be rebuked as if he had committed a great sin. **2.** Nor shall a man decide in favour of any man related to him, whether father, or son, or brother, or any of their relations, in accordance with the commandments which our fathers have decreed for us, without having been sent or having asked. **3.** Nor shall any man speak inside the infirmary while sitting and eating or drinking the small portion needful, but they shall drink it sensibly and in the fear of God. For are they at a banquet or in a tavern that they will talk so much in that place? **4.** Where is the wisdom? Where is the understanding? Where is the fear of God? I testify to you that there are many who, though in need, are oblivious because of the fear of God and bear in mind the resting-places which are in the kingdom of heaven. **5.** And there are many who of necessity ask for their needs and, receiving them with weeping and sadness, bear in mind the punishments and remember the brethren who have gone to God striving. They did not ask for such a thing, but rather remember what is written, 'Through many tribulations we shall enter the kingdom of God' [47].

X. **1.** But as for us, do not let us ask for our needs dishonestly, saying that we are sick when we are not sick, but let us ask for our needs truthfully in the fear of God. **2.** And let us not be deceived by a surfeiting of the belly [48] and ask without being in need, lest God be angry with us and cast us together with those who work lawlessness, as it is written, 'Those who turn aside to these dishonest dealings the Lord will cast together with those who work law-

[46] Cf. Deut. 27. 15 etc. [47] Acts 14. 22. [48] Cf. Prov. 24. 15.

lessness'[49]. **3.** For who prevents him who is really sick from asking truthfully? Or whose heart shall be able to withstand if he sees one who is genuinely sick when he is in need? And no one among those who go there, asking for their needs, shall taste of the small helping needful to his neighbour, while saying in their ignorant hearts, 'This is better than ours', or, 'This man's is better than this man's'. **4.** For they shall not be like those who favour one another, but * that which each one shall receive, he shall drink *p. 37 sensibly, and no one shall be a respecter of persons in that place. **5.** He who talks in that place over and above what is fitting, shall be rebuked in accordance with the rules of our fathers. **6.** For as it is laid down that no man shall speak in the refectory, but if they lack anything they shall knock sensibly, so is it also in that place. For this is an eating-place and the other one is an eating-place too.

XI. **1.** Therefore, brethren, let us fear God. For he who fears the Lord will guard himself from everything, but he who does not fear shall be in places, the Eternal One not visiting him[50]. **2.** Moreover, we despise the commandments of God because of our passions; or else we are found bursting the bonds which God has made in heaven that they may, through our fathers, have their being upon earth. **3.** These are reliable commandments for those who desire their salvation, and unbreakable commandments for those who love life, which our fathers have inflexibly decreed for us, so that those who transgress them shall be rebuked according to their deserts. **4.** And not only this, but they shall also render account to God. In particular, he who dares to do any such thing from to-day on shall be greatly cursed. **5.** But he who takes care not to transgress shall be blessed. However, as it is written, 'It is not a new commandment which is given to you but it is an old commandment which is decreed for us from the beginning'[51]. **6.** And the Lord Christ Jesus will give power to everyone who keeps his words and his commandments, and he will bless them with all their works.

[49] Ps. 124. 5. [50] Cf. Prov. 19. 20. — The last clause should perhaps be emended to read : 'which the Eternal One does not visit', as in Prov. 19. 20, cf. also p. 10 where it is accurately quoted, but cf. p. 46. [51] Cf. I Jn. 2. 7.

[Fragment 13] *TO APHTHONIA*

I. **1.** Did you indeed give glory to God?[1] I am talking to you, Aphthonia, daughter of the *comes* Alexandros. Or did you honour the place in which you were nurtured according to God and according to the world, with your words and your deeds?[2] **2.** If your heart had not been corrupt, you would not have despised the place in which you are, nor would you have disgraced the sisters who * p. 38 are there with you. **3.** * You are indeed called by your name Aphthonia, but you bear malice against yourself, and you are slanderous of yourself[3]. You want to destroy your soul which the whole world is not worth[4] and to lose your sufferings for naught, for you gave Satan opportunity within you to turn your heart and bewilder you like rotten sheep. **4.** Senseless and ignorant one, who is without wisdom! For if there were any sense in you, even if they had really opposed you, is it proper for you to appoint people to know how you are getting on in your convent? **5.** In particular, you have sent to your father and your mother, 'They have opposed me', or, 'They have abused me'. You are lying for they have not opposed you nor have they abused you. They opposed you in that they instilled sense into you when you transgressed the commandment and received something from your parents without asking. **6.** What is it that you were seeking after that you need? Was it refused or was it not given to you? If you inform your father and your mother, are we afraid? Especially as you are lying. Do you want us then to report to them the follies you perpetrate and your thefts and your quarrels?

II. **1.** Truly, blind one who is groping at noonday like those at midnight and like the blind who have no eyes[5], how is it that your parents outside in the world shall hear your speech inside this place and we, in the convent, shall not know? **2.** If you were really ill-treated or ill-used or grieved, you ought to tell us your sorrow that we may know whether or not you speak the truth, or to tell your mother who is there with you, if you do not call her mother only with your mouth; but your heart is

1 Possibly a sarcastic statement. 2 Possibly a sarcastic statement. 3 Cf. perhaps Gal. 3. 1 (Sah. and Greek). 4 Cf. Mt. 16. 26, Mk. 8. 36, Heb. 11. 38. 5 Cf. Is. 59. 10.

far from her, as it is written, 'This people honours me with their lips but their heart is far from me'[6]. **3.** For if your ignorant heart had not been darkened in you, would you have despised your fathers who are in the community with you, or would you have scorned the sisters with whom you live, in your pride and your boastfulness? **4.** Or if you had not forsaken the teaching and the wisdom, and loved the evil more than the good[7], would you have declaimed wicked words and said with your mouth which is full of cursing and bitterness[8], 'I shall go to another convent'? **5.** Wherein has this place * ill-treated you? Or what is the burden which was laid * p. 39 upon you, except that you were told not to transgress the commandment of God, because you gave perfume and nard[9] to a young girl with you in the house, that you might become a hindrance and a stumbling-block to each other? **6.** Therefore I promise you : if you do not take to yourself understanding and put this disobedience from you and these pointless quarrels, I shall make your heart sorrowful, and I shall cause there to be done to you according to that which has come out of your mouth.

III. **1.** Truly, I am troubled at heart within myself about you and you (all). I fear lest, as the serpent beguiled Eve in his craftiness, your hearts should be corrupted from the simplicity and the purity which lead towards Christ[10]. **2.** If he did not leave that one in paradise, will he spare you or you (all) when you give him opportunity amongst you and receive to yourselves his deceitful counsels and his wicked works? For he shall not prevail over those who fear God, those for whom Christ is a helper and protector[10a],

[6] Mt. 15. 8, Mk. 7. 6, cf. Is. 29. 13. [7] Cf. Ps. 51. 5. [8] Cf. Ps. 9. 28, Rom. 3. 14. [9] Meaning and etymology unknown, cf. CRUM, *Dictionary*, 187 b. The context suggests some kind of cosmetic. Is it possible that the word is connected with μεσόσφαιρος, -ον, 'of middle globular size', cf. H. G. LIDDELL and R. SCOTT, *A Greek-English Lexicon*, Oxford, 1951, p. 1108a. Sophocles (*Greek Lexicon of the Roman and Byzantine Periods*, London, 1888) gives as the meaning of μεσόσφαιρον 'the middle-sized μαλάβαθρον' (μαλάβαθρον = the aromatic leaf of an Indian tree; cf. also the Latin *mesosphaerum* = a kind of nard with middle-sized leaves). Skarlatos (Λεξικὸν τῆς ἑλληνικῆς γλώσσης, Athens, 1852) suggests betel as an equivalent of μαλάβαθρον. If this is the correct derivation of **ⲙⲉⲥⲟⲩⲁⲫⲓ**, the meaning here may be either an aromatic ointment, or else a masticatory preparation, perhaps with the additional property of reddening the lips and gums. [10] II Cor. 11. 3. [10a] Cf. Ex. 15. 2.

as it is written, 'He who fights for you is your helper and he is the sword of your pride[11] and the glory of the firmament'[12]. **3.** He who loves the evil will perish, and over him will the devil prevail by his soul-destroying works. But the wise man who loves instruction shall take to himself the commandment[13], and the prudent who fears the Lord shall acquire for himself guidance[14]. **4.** In any case, let me hear that you have set at ease your fathers who are there with you, and that you have obeyed them in everything, so that our heart may be at ease and you too may enjoy contentment. **5.** Moreover, if you have anything to say, here are the elders, our fathers and our brethren; they have come to you, tell it to them. And all of you, if you have a point to raise[15] or anything in your convent, do not stop without telling them and do not hide anything from them, that all our hearts may be at ease together, ours and yours, and that the Lord too may be content with us.

[Fragment 14] *TO ANTINOE*

* p. 40 * Besa writes to Antinoe.

I. **1.** God is holy who dwells amongst the saints, who finds rest amongst the saints, who gives patience to the fainthearted, and who gives life to the broken-hearted[1]. So God shall find rest through them, and they shall find rest the more through him. **2.** For amongst men who perform the commandments of the Lord and keep them, he finds rest and blesses them greatly, and shelters them from every evil that the enemy shall not prevail over them. **3.** Therefore, it is fitting for us to reflect and to consider, and not to be ignorant that the things we promised to God were no longer ours but God's. **4.** May it come to pass that the Lord give you the means to pray to him even as it has been said, 'Create in me a pure heart, O God, and let a right spirit be renewed within me'[1a]. And, 'Cast me not away from your face and take not your holy spirit from me'[2].

II. **1.** For indeed, our Lord Jesus Christ, our Saviour, wished that all men should live, and that they should come to the knowledge of the truth, even as he calls everyone to life, saying, 'Come to me all who are weary and laden and I shall give you rest. Take

11 Cf. Deut. 33. 29. 12 Deut. 33. 26. 13 Cf. Prov. 10. 8. 14 Cf. Prov. 1. 5. 15 Lit. : 'word'.

1 Cf. Is. 57. 15. 1a Ps. 50. 12. 2 Ps. 50. 13.

my yoke upon you and learn of me, for I am meek and humble in my heart, and you shall find rest for your souls. For my yoke is sweet and my burden light'[3]. **2.** For what is sweeter than the law of God, or what is lighter than his commandments? This means that he calls us with his truthful mouth saying, 'He who wishes to be perfect, let him sell all his possessions and give them to the poor, and lay up for himself a treasure in heaven, and come and follow me'[4]. **3.** And he also adds to the saying, confirming all who believe in him and who have followed him with their whole heart, and, encouraging them, he says, 'Fear not, little flock, for your Father wishes to give you the kingdom. Sell your belongings, give them for charity, and make for yourselves purses which do not grow old, * and an unfailing treasure in heaven where no thief approaches, and no moth destroys it'[5]. **4.** Likewise, all our blessed fathers who have gone to God, and we, our miserable selves, have also wished that you may benefit your soul and that you may obtain this great good of which God has made you worthy, and that you may not put it

* p. 41

[Fragment 15] *ON LACK OF FOOD*

I. **1.** you are suffering with those who are bound[1], which means those who are afflicted in their manner of living on the herbs of the field, in that they have not found that which they may eat, even as we hear and those who see confirm their suffering. **2.** Therefore, let us all pray, everyone who fears God, that Christ should make his blessing abide on his communities and that he should not permit his monasteries to lack anything.

[Fragment 16] *ON A FAMINE*

O Lord, my God, I will glorify you and I will bless your name, for you are wonderful in your glories, performing marvels[1].

I. **1.** You are blessed, O Lord God Almighty, Father of our Lord Jesus Christ, who is blessed and yet more blessed eternally; who is before the ages; who has created the heavens and all that is therein, the sovereignties, the authorities, the powers, the

[3] Mt. 11. 28-30. [4] Cf. Mt. 19. 21. [5] Lk. 12. 32-33.

[1] Cf. perhaps Heb. 10. 34.

[1] Cf. Is. 25. 1.

dominions [1a], the cherubim, the seraphim, the earth, the sea, the rivers, and your whole creation which you have made. **2.** You are blessed in all your works and all your ordinances, Creator of all, for you have made us worthy that this great good should happen to us in this year, namely the ninth. **3.** In the sixth year since our reverend father, Apa Shenoute, died, in the seventh month, on the twelfth day of the month [2], when a great calamity had occurred in the whole land with famines and diseases, when this great multitude gathered at this place, having fallen sick, and many of whom died.

* p. 42 II. **1.** * Thanks be to God that the brethren attended them. They cared for them in everything. They did not leave them lacking anything in all their necessity that they need, either gruel, food, fresh or salted pigeon, eggs, cheese, to wash them, or to give medicine to those with sores. **2.** In short the brethren did not leave them lacking anything that they need at all, not by our strength but by the grace of God, our Saviour, who gave himself a ransom for everyone [3]. **3.** They served the sick and all the multitudes also for whom they daily prepared that they might be fed. There would be more than five thousand people or six thousand, sometimes more than these or (sometimes) less. **4.** And all those who died, being more than one hundred and twenty-eight people, were cared for; they buried them with everything necessary through the blessing of Christ Jesus, our Lord, who gave power to the brethren while they ministered to them, until the district was relieved and each one went to his place.

III. **1.** Therefore, we confess to you, our Lord Jesus Christ, and your blessed Father, that all your deeds are justice and your deeds are just judgements, for all these things have happened because of our sins. **2.** And our lawlessnesses have turned away from us what are your mercies, and our sins have caused the good things to be far from us, and our iniquities and our wickednesses have caused you to turn your face from us, so as

1a Cf. perhaps Eph. 1. 21. 2 I.e. March 8th; this system of dating does not allow the year to be determined exactly, but the famine probably occurred either in A.D. 456 or in A.D. 471, which are both 9th years of Indiction periods. Cf. my article 'A Fifth-Century Egyptian Abbot', *The Journal of Theological Studies*, N.S.V, p. 38. 3 I Tim. 2. 6.

not to have pity on us. And you have delivered us to every tribulation, namely death and famine and every affliction. **3.** In all these things our heart still did not perceive that we should turn and fear you and call upon your name, for you are a merciful God, repenting of the evils [4]. **4.** O Lord, our God, forgive us, and grant us to turn from our wickednesses, and consider in all righteousness and in all truth, and do good in your sight. **5.** Hear us, Lord, for your mercy is good [5]; forgive us, Lord; be merciful, Lord. Pay heed, Lord, to our suffering and our sorrow and the distress of the whole world. Do it for your own sake, and delay not, Lord, our God. **6.** For who else is God except you, who takes away the lawlessnesses and overlooks our iniquities [6] and * our transgressions; because you are compassionate and you are long-suffering, great is your mercy [7]. **7.** For all these sufferings have befallen us because we disobeyed you, even as you have spoken through the prophet, 'All these things have befallen you because of me, you shall lie down in sorrow' [8]. So therefore we were filled with tears.

* p. 43

IV. **1.** Woe to us for we have sinned! That is why our heart was grieved [9]. And woe to us because we have not learned to follow you, and we have not ceased from our wicked works, in order that good may befall us. **2.** Yours is the righteousness, O Lord; ours is the shamefacedness [10], even as in this day. **3.** Mercies and forgivenesses are yours, Lord Jesus, for we have sinned in everything and have departed from you. We have not obeyed your voice, and your commandments, and your injunctions which you enjoined on us, that we should walk in them [11], in order that good may befall us. **4.** But we walked in the desire of our evil heart, until all these sufferings have come upon us. Our disobedience will teach us and our wickedness will upbraid us. Know and let us see that it is bitter for us to forsake the law of God [12] and his statutes and his commandments. **5.** Help us, Lord Jesus, God, our Saviour, for the glory of your name, Lord, save us, and forgive our lawlessnesses for your name's sake; lest the unbelievers and the pagans say,

[4] Cf. Jonah 4. 2. [5] Cf. Ps. 68. 17. [6] Cf. Mic. 7. 18. [7] Jonah 4. 2. [8] Is. 50. 11. [9] Lam. 5. 16-17. [10] Dan. (θ) 9. 8. [11] Cf. Dan. (θ) 9. 9-10. [12] Cf. Jer. 2. 19.

'Where is their God?'[13] But save us in accordance with your wonders, and glorify your name, Lord. **6.** Remember not our former lawlessnesses[14], but let there be a pure heart in us and let a right spirit be renewed within us[15], and make us worthy that a spirit of discernment may live in us, that we may discern between the good and the evil[16]. **7.** Lord, remember us and visit us[17], and make us worthy that your mercies reach us quickly for we have become very poor[18]. Men and beasts shall you save, O Lord[19]. **8.** Lord, your compassion is eternal, do not forsake the works of your hands[20] Remember your mercies, Lord, and your compassions for they are from of old[21].

* p. 44 V. **1.** * Behold, therefore, our unworthiness and our obstinate sins have robbed us of your yearly mercy, which is the inundation of the river. **2.** It is in your power every day but our sins deprive us of the good things and, because of our wickednesses, you have turned your face from us so as not to have mercy on us. **3.** Therefore, woe to us because we fled from you; misery shall overtake us because we did iniquity against you[22]. For on this it has been said, 'How long shall the land mourn, and all the grass of the field wither for the wickedness of those who live in the land? The birds and the beasts perished; they said, "God shall not see our ways" '[23]. **4.** What (profit) is it to us that these things befall us? Our heart errs and our lawlessness engulfs us; our soul has fallen into fearfulness[24]. **5.** For our lawlessnesses are in us and we have known our iniquities. We did iniquity, we lied, and we ceased from following after our God[25]. We conceived and uttered from our heart iniquitous words. We turned backwards judgement and righteousness was far off, because truth perished in their ways and they were unable to go through the straight[26]. **6.** Therefore the curse shall devour the land because those who live therein have sinned[27].

VI. **1.** But if our sins have stood against us, Lord, work for us for your name's sake because our sins are many before you, for we have sinned against you[28]. **2.** Teach us, Lord, but with judgement,

13 Cf. Ps. 78. 9-10. 14 Ps. 78. 8. 15 Cf. Ps. 50. 12. 16 Cf. Heb. 5. 14. 17 Cf. Jer. 15. 15. 18 Ps. 78. 8. 19 Ps. 35. 7. 20 Ps. 137. 8. 21 Ps. 24. 6. 22 Cf. Hos. 7. 13. 23 Jer. 12. 4. 24 Cf. Is. 21. 4. 25 Is. 59. 12-13. 26 Is. 59. 13-14. 27 Is. 24. 6. 28 Jer. 14. 7.

not with your anger, lest you cause us to diminish [29]. Do to us according to your pity and according to the multitude of your mercies [30], because you are a merciful God. **3.** Lord, our God, remember us and visit us [31]. Do not do to us according to our sins and do not requite us according to our lawlessnesses [32]. For if you pay heed to our iniquities and our transgressions, who shall be able to stand [33], because forgiveness is with you? [34] For if you open your hand [35] ... *1 folio missing* ...

[Fragment 17] *ADMONITIONS TO SINNERS*

I. **1.** despised, in that we did not fear while we are always commanded and exhorted by the Lord, 'Watch'. Watch for what? * We are told to guard ourselves so as not to sin. **2.** We remember * p. 45
with fear what he said, 'Watch, for you know not the day nor the hour [1] wherein we shall be visited'. **3.** Even as he also says, 'Watch, for you know not when your Lord comes, whether at eventide, or at midnight, or at the hour of cockcrow, or at the morning hour [2]; lest he come suddenly and find you sleeping. What I say to you', he said, 'I say to all, "Watch" ' [3]. **4.** The men of Nineveh were, once upon a time, preached to by a single prophet. He did not speak to them a multitude of words and he did not instil fear into them concerning the punishments which are to come, and he did not preach to them the good tidings of the resting-places which are in the kingdom of heaven until they repented; but he said to them only, 'Yet three days and Nineveh shall be destroyed' [4]. **5.** And they believed [5] and feared the word of the prophet which he had spoken, lest they should die miserably. Therefore, they turned quickly from their wickednesses and the iniquity which is in their hands [6]. **6.** They proclaimed a fast [7], acceptable to God, and prayed and entreated, saying in their heart, 'Who knows whether God will repent and turn from the anger of his wrath and we die not' [8]. **7.** So the Lord saw their repentance, how they turned with all

29 Jer. 10. 24. 30 Cf. Ps. 50. 3. 31 Cf. Jer. 15. 15. 32 Cf. Ps. 102. 10.
33 Cf. Ps. 129. 3. 34 Ps. 129. 4. 35 Cf. Ps. 103. 28.

1 Mt. 25. 13. 2 Cf. Mk. 13. 35. 3 Mk. 13. 36-37. 4 Jonah 3. 4.
5 Cf. Jonah 3. 5. 6 Cf. Jonah 3. 8. 7 Cf. Jonah 3. 5. 8 Jonah 3. 9.

their heart. He had mercy on them. He revoked his decision so as not to destroy them [9].

II. **1.** But to us witness is borne and promise is made of the good things which are in the kingdom of God, and to us a multitude of words is proclaimed from all the scriptures, and by our Lord Jesus in the gospels, and by our fathers in their teachings which they command us. **2.** Yet we had no regret so as to turn and repent and hate the evil and love the good [10], lest we die in our sins and God have no mercy upon us to let compassion reach us in that place, because we were told and did not hear, and we did not perceive so as to pay heed to teaching and prepare our ears for the words of
* p. 46 knowledge [11]. **3.** It has been said, 'Because of food do not * destroy the work of God' [12]. Therefore, because of evil aspirations, in which there is no profit, do not let us destroy the fear of Christ and the work of God, lest we repent on the day of the righteous judgement of God, which is a sentence completing and cutting short, which God will execute [13] on that day. **4.** Concerning this (day) it has been said, 'That day is a day of wrath; it is a day of tribulation and anguish [14] for those who have not prepared themselves that compassion might reach them on that day and in that hour'. But the wise man shall acquire for himself guidance [15].

III. **1.** So then, holy brethren, partakers of the heavenly calling [16], if our sins will not make us unworthy, we pray and beseech you in the Lord Jesus Christ, and we adjure you by the heaven and the earth to depart from the unfruitful works of darkness but rather reprove them [17]. **2.** Concerning these it has been said, 'For the things they do in secret are disgraceful even to mention' [18], which are pollution, defilement, theft, and lying, of which it has been said, 'The wrath of God is coming because of them' [19]. **3.** And it has also been said, 'Wash your heart from wickedness, Jerusalem, that you may be saved' [20]. But we washed away righteousness and sowed in ourselves wickednesses and evils [21], as it is written, 'The foolish shall share wickedness among themselves' [22]. And, 'He who kindles wickedness shall perish therein' [23]. **4.** And again, 'He who

[9] Cf. Jonah 3. 10. [10] Cf. Amos 5. 15. [11] Cf. Prov. 23. 12. [12] Rom. 14. 20. [13] Rom. 9. 28. [14] Zeph. 1. 15. [15] Prov. 1. 5. [16] Heb. 3. 1. [17] Eph. 5. 11. [18] Eph. 5. 12. [19] Cf. Eph. 5. 6. [20] Jer. 4. 14. [21] Cf. p. 81. [22] Prov. 14. 18. [23] Prov. 19. 6.

goads with words shall not be saved'[24]. And again, 'Those who walk in a way which is not good, but have followed after their sins[25]; this people which provokes me to anger to my face[26]. And they have chosen their ways and their iniquities and their abominations which their soul desired'[27]. **5.** Therefore it has also been said, 'I also will choose their wantonnesses and I will repay them their sins; for I called them and they did not hear me, I spoke and they did not listen; they did evil in my sight and they chose the things which I do not wish'[28].

IV. **1.** Therefore, woe to the disobedient sons, for they are in utter perdition with flabby hands and slackened knees, concerning which the apostle has said, 'Restore * the flabby hands and the slackened knees and make straight paths for your feet, that that which is lame should not be turned aside but rather be healed'[29]. **2.** For on this it has been said, 'There are six things which the Lord has hated and seven are abominations to his soul[30] : a scorner's eye, an iniquitous tongue, hands which shed righteous blood[31], feet which hasten to do evil[32], a perverted heart[33], an unstable conduct, winkings of the eye, beckonings with the finger, signallings with their feet[34], quarrellings, and disobediences'. **3.** Especially do they despise their fathers with their boastfulness, and their arrogance, and their contempt, for they did not remember that which is written, 'He who despises his father and his mother shall be under reproach and be ashamed'[35]. **4.** And again, 'He who ill-treats his father and his mother, and he who despises them thinking, "I do not sin", is an associate of an ungodly man'[36]. **5.** And again, 'The light of him who reviles his father and his mother shall go out, the pupils of his eyes shall see darkness'[37]. **6.** And again, 'He who shall revile his father and his mother, let him die the death'[38].

* p. 47

V. **1.** But, in particular, those who care for clothes by embroider-

24 Prov. 19. 4. 25 Cf. Is. 65. 2. 26 Is. 65. 3. 27 Cf. Is. 66. 3. 28 Is. 66. 4. 29 Heb. 12. 12-13. 30 Prov. 6. 17. — This, though not in the LXX, is in the Sah. (W. H. Worrell, *The Proverbs of Solomon in Sahidic Coptic*, Chicago, 1931), cf. also Prov. 6. 16 in the Hebrew text. 31 Prov. 6. 17. 32 Prov. 6. 18. 33 Cf. Prov. 6. 14. 34 Cf. Prov. 6. 13. 35 Cf. Prov. 19. 23. 36 Cf. Prov. 28. 24. 37 Prov. 20. 10. 38 Cf. Ex. 21. 16, Lev. 20. 9, Mt. 15. 4, Mk. 7. 10.

ing them, such are those of whom it is said, 'For they set their house near death and their paths near hell'[39]; and of those it has also been said, 'But the ways of the ungodly are dark, and they do not know how they stumble'[40]. **2.** And again, 'They did not know nor did they understand, they walk in darkness'[41]. And they were not afraid of the curse which is written for us concerning these things, but they even provoke God to anger with all their works, that he, the Lord of glory, for his part, will mock them in the fiery furnace which burns in hell on the day of their visitation. **3.** For thus when he saw that we are not upright and that there is no stability in us nor truth nor knowledge of God,
* p. 48 he said, 'I said, "You are gods, * all of you sons of the Highest. But, behold, you shall die like men and you shall fall like one of the princes" '[42]. **4.** This means that we are thought to be faithful and godly men, filled with every good thing. If we are seen to be unstable, it will be said of us thus, 'We think that you are men who fear God. But, behold, your way is our way, and your deeds are our deeds'. **5.** Behold, therefore, you shall die like godless men and sinners, and you shall fall like iniquitous princes[43] and the foundations of the earth shall be moved[44]. This means men simply as they are. **6.** And they will be amazed at our disgrace and the misfortune which has befallen us, for we changed our nature into that which is against nature[45].

VI. **1.** But the Lord Jesus will save us from this curse which is written, 'And when they had become impious, they hated knowledge and became liable to reproofs'[46]. **2.** And it has also been said, 'He who loves instruction loves knowledge, but he who hates reproofs is a fool'[47]. **3.** Therefore, brethren, let us pay heed to the word which is written, 'Listen, my son, to the instruction of your father that you may become wise at your end'[48]. **4.** And again, 'Be wise, my son, that my heart may rejoice, and turn away from you shameful words[49] that you may have confidence in God'[50]. For the fear of the Lord works for life, but he who does not fear shall be in places; the Eternal One does not visit him[51].

[39] Cf. Prov. 2. 18. [40] Prov. 4. 19. [41] Ps. 81. 5. [42] Ps. 81. 6-7. [43] Cf. Ps. 81. 7. [44] Cf. Ps. 81. 5. [45] Cf. Rom. 1. 26. [46] Prov. 1. 22-23. [47] Prov. 12. 1. [48] Prov. 19. 17. [49] Prov. 27. 11. [50] Prov. 22. 19. [51] Cf. Prov. 19. 20. — The last clause should perhaps be emended to read :

5. Wicked men and disobedient sons, stiff-necked and uncircumcised in heart and ears too [52], will you not then fear the Lord, or will you not be in awe before him? [53] **6.** Therefore, disobedient men and such as do not fear the Lord, cease from your stubborn disobedience and circumcise your stubborn heart and do not again be stiff-necked, lest God be angry with you and cast you together with those who work lawlessness [54]. **7.** For if you do not fear now and * depart from the hardness of your heart, there shall be a day when we shall break our heart and weep bitterly with no one to hear us, because we did not weep at the proper time. * p. 49

VII. **1.** For all who steal now, and who lie, and who defile themselves in any way, and who embroider their garments in demonic passions, shall be cursed with all their works, because they did not fear the Lord and did not pay heed, though being commanded at all times about these disgraceful and foul things. For those who do such things shall be fettered in their wicked thoughts [55]. **2.** Therefore, let all of us together pay attention to how we are told, 'The night is far spent, the day is at hand, let us therefore forsake the works of darkness and put upon us the armour of light. As being in the day, let us walk decently, not in revellings and drunkennesses, in immoral intercourses [56] ... *2 folios missing ...*

[Fragment 18] *TO SINFUL NUNS*

I. **1.** evil [and we] turn and repent, and know whence we are, as it has been said, 'Who will give heed to become thus therein' [1], that we may also become worthy to say confidently, 'Tribulations you have shown me many times and evils, and you have turned

'which the Eternal One does not visit', as in Prov. 19. 20, cf. also p. 10 where it is accurately quoted, but cf. p. 35. [52] Acts 7. 51. [53] Cf. Jer. 5. 22. [54] Cf. Ps. 124. 5. [55] Cf. Prov. 20. 14. [56] Rom. 13. 12-13.

[1] Cf. Deut. 5. 29. — Perhaps emend to read : 'Who will give to their heart that it becomes thus in them'. The literal translation in the LXX, and thence in the Coptic version of Deut., of the Hebrew Desiderative Sentence ('O that they had such an heart!', cf. E. KAUTZSCH, *Gesenius' Hebrew Grammar*, Second English Edition, Oxford, 1952, § 151 c) has given rise to this obscurity.

and quickened me; you have brought me up from the depths of the earth. You have [increased your greatness upon me and you have turned and comforted me'[2]. **2.** And again, 'The Lord has heard], he had mercy upon me[3]. He turned my mourning for me into joy'[4]. And again, 'He has torn off my sackcloth, he has girded me with gladness'[5]. And again, 'Weeping shall be in the evening and rejoicing in the morning'[6]. **3.** Who is wise and knows these things? and prudent and understands them? For the ways of the Lord are straight[7]. ... *6 lines missing* ... [and those which] come after the words which the Lord has spoken in his teaching. He
* p. 50 used to call and to say, 'He who has ears to hear, * let him hear'[8]. **4.** For what man has no ears? But he says, 'He who has understanding to perceive and to hear, let him hear and be sober unto ... *3 lines missing* ... and let us be sober unto the things which our fathers command us, in order that we may profit and have stability. **5.** For a pasture of righteousness belongs to the congregation of our fathers[9], that those who wish and those with knowledge may walk in this salvation, as it is written; which means the hearing and keeping of the commandments.

II. **1.** And you all together, let each woman obey your fathers in everything, that their hearts may be at rest and that you too may be filled with contentment. **2.** 'And let your loins be girded, your lamps burning'[10], even as the Lord has said, 'and be you like these men who look out for their lord, when he will return from the marriage; that if he come and knock, they shall open to him at once'[11]. **3.** He has said, 'Blessed are those servants whom their lord, on coming, finds vigilant'[12]. And again he has said, 'Verily, I say to you that he will gird himself and make them recline, and come forth and minister to them. And if he should come in the second watch or the third and find them doing thus, blessed are those servants'[13]. **4.** For also the five wise virgins, who were found vigilant and with oil in their vessels, not having let their lamps be extinguished, are they who entered with the bridegroom. **5.** But as for them, the negligent and foolish ones

2 Ps. 70. 20-21. 3 Ps. 29. 11. 4 Ps. 29. 12. 5 Ps. 29. 12. 6 Ps. 29. 6.
7 Hos. 14. 10. 8 Mt. 11. 15 etc. 9 Cf. Jer. 27. 7. 10 Lk. 12. 35.
11 Lk. 12. 36. 12 Lk. 12. 37. 13 Lk. 12. 37-38.

who did not prepare oil in their vessels that their lamps might burn, they did not enter with him. But they stood outside the door entreating, 'Open to us'. It was not opened[14]. And not only did he say to them, 'I know you not'[15], but he said, 'there shall be weeping and gnashing of teeth'[16].

III. **1.** So then, do not let us also be negligent lest these things befall us, but let us be sober and vigilant[17] on every side, for it has been said, 'The end of all is nigh. Be prudent therefore and be sober unto prayers[18], and let us become wise in respect of good, but innocent in respect of evil[19], as if we knew it * not, * p. 51 lest it destroy our good heart'. **2.** As the apostle has said, 'For I was ready to present you as a pure virgin to one husband, Christ. But I fear lest, as the serpent beguiled Eve in his craftiness, your hearts should be corrupted from the simplicity and the purity which lead towards Christ'[20]. **3.** Thus our fathers are troubled at heart for us and they are afraid always, in order that we may escape and be saved from the snares of the devil who envies us and acts wickedly against those who desire their salvation. **4.** For on this subject we were commanded and charged strictly, 'Be sober and vigilant because your adversary goes, roaring as the lions, seeking to devour your souls'[21]. **5.** For we have been taught thus, 'The fear of the Lord is the beginning of wisdom'[22]. And, 'Understanding is good for all who practise it'[23]. **6.** And again it is said, 'The wise man in his works is a finder of good things'[24].

IV. **1.** Therefore, let us acquire for ourselves the fear of the Lord and understanding, that they may guard us from every evil thing, and let us escape like a gazelle out of a snare and like a bird out of a trap[25]. **2.** For the Lord calls us and entreats us as children, saying, 'Come, my children, and hearken unto me and I will teach you the fear of the Lord. Who is the man', it has been said, 'who desires the life and loves to see good days?[26] **3.** Let him make his tongue cease from evil and his lips from speaking guile. Let him turn away from the evil and do the good, let him seek peace and

[14] Cf. Mt. 25. 1 ff. [15] Mt. 25. 12. [16] Lk. 13. 28. [17] Cf. I Thes. 5. 6, I Pet. 5. 8. [18] I Pet. 4. 7. [19] Cf. Rom. 16. 19. [20] II Cor. 11. 2-3. [21] I Pet. 5. 8. [22] Prov. 1. 7. [23] Prov. 1. 7. [24] Prov. 16. 20. [25] Cf. Prov. 6. 5. [26] Ps. 33. 12-13.

pursue it [27]. **4.** For the eyes of the Lord look upon the righteous and his ears are turned to their prayer [28], so that he may do them good and that he may save them from the devil, that he may not prevail over them with his accursed sins. **5.** But the face of the Lord is upon those who do wickednesses to blot out their remembrance from upon the earth [29], and to deliver them into the hand of Satan to punish them with every tribulation', as it has been said, 'Whom I delivered unto Satan that he should teach them' [30]. **6.** So then, * p. 52 sisters, whether great or small, let us look * to ourselves, and flee from the things which God hates, which are pollution, theft, lying, fighting, quarrelling, and hatred, that you may not grieve yourselves now, and grieve yourselves the more on the day when we shall stand at the judgement-seat of Christ and each man and each woman shall receive according to our works in respect of the things we have done, whether good or evil [31]. **7.** And (let us look to ourselves) lest it be as the apostle said, 'Lest by any means I should come to you and find you not as I wish, and you should find me not as you wish me; lest', he said, 'by any means there should be strifes, jealousies, wraths, provocations, evil-speakings, whisperings, vanities, disturbances [32], pollutions, and thefts'. **8.** He says, 'Lest by any means I come and find these things among you and you grieve me' [33], and I, for my part, cause your heart to be troubled as you do not wish.

V. **1.** Now therefore, sisters, be vigilant and prepare yourselves in every good work and we shall find means to meet one another contentedly, lest, instead of seeing one another to advantage with satisfaction, we, on the other hand, come to you in grief, sorrow, and sighing. **2.** But let us stand in our ways and see and seek the eternal ways of the Lord, and see which is the good way, and walk in it, and you will find purification for your souls [34], lest it is said of us too, 'They are hungry and thirsty [35]; they did not find the way of the city of their habitation' [36]. **3.** Do not think, sisters, that we say these things in hatred of one another, but we take much thought for one another, desiring our sound establishment and our

[27] Cf. Ps. 33. 14-15. [28] Ps. 33. 16. [29] Ps. 33. 17. [30] I Tim. 1. 20.
[31] Cf. II Cor. 5. 10. [32] II Cor. 12. 20. [33] Cf. perhaps II Cor. 12. 21.
[34] Cf. Jer. 6. 16. [35] Ps. 106. 5. [36] Ps. 106. 4.

steadfastness. **4.** Therefore, we say them in sadness and sighings and sorrowings, that we may know how, we walk in the household of God, and that you may know the love which we have abundantly towards you, your fathers, your brethren, your sons, and your daughters together. **5.** For we do not want anyone to perish from amongst us or lose his sufferings for naught, and we are troubled at heart concerning those who hate themselves and act wickedly against themselves because of their obstinacy and their disobedience. **6.** And we also wish that we should examine ourselves, and know and understand * that it is a fearful thing to fall into the hands of * p. 53 the living God[37]. **7.** And again, 'It is a fearful thing to expect the judgement and the fierceness[38] of the fire which will devour the adversaries'[39]. Who are the adversaries of whom mention is made except those who sin against God and who bear malice against themselves and who invalidate their own sufferings? **8.** 'Therefore', it has been said, 'be not foolish, but know what the will of the Lord is'[40], and that which comes after this. And, 'Look how you walk, not as foolish but as wise[41], buying the time, for the days are evil'[42]. **9.** Nevertheless, here are our fathers and our brethren; they have come to you in the love of God. Do not hide from them anything in your midst, whether concerning those who quarrel, or those who are disobedient, or any evil thing, that they may come to us contentedly.

[Fragment 19] *ON THE SINFULNESS OF THE COMMUNITY*

You are righteous, Lord, therefore I shall speak before you[1].

I. **1.** O this great sorrow and this immense, still-unceasing grief from the false brethren who feared not God and did not remember their end, but added sin upon sin because of their disobedience and their evil works! **2.** They have made up their mind not to believe, and they have shut their ears so as not to hear the words of God and the commandments of our fathers. **3.** How long do we oppose the word which is written in our disobedience, 'You scourged them and they were not grieved; you destroyed them

[37] Heb. 10. 31. [38] Cf. p. 8, n. 35. [39] Heb. 10. 27. [40] Eph. 5. 17. [41] Cf. Eph. 5. 15. [42] Eph. 5. 16.

[1] Jer. 12. 1.

and they did not want to receive instruction'[1a] ? **4.** Or do we lack that God disciplines us with various infirmities as a father teaches his children so that our stubborn heart should be humble and we should turn to him in repentance and that he should have mercy upon our wretchedness and remove these sufferings from us. **5.** Yet we did not realise that we should depart from the evil and do the good[2]. How long, therefore, do we draw down upon us * p. 54 the judgement of these words, ' "Will you not fear * me", says the Lord, "or will you not be in awe before me" '?[3] **6.** For on this, when the Lord saw us persisting in our obstinacy and our wickednesses, he speaks to us thus, 'If you approach me treacherously and do not wish to obey me, I will add seven plagues to you according to your sins[4]. And I will crush the disdain of your arrogance'[5]. **7.** Then again, 'And after these things, if you are not taught but approach me treacherously, I also will walk with you in wrath treacherously, and I will also strike you seven times for your sins'[6]. **8.** How long are we to be in these evils not having purified ourselves so as to follow the Lord, our God, with repentance and weeping and sighing, in order that he may forgive us, and have compassion on us, and turn his wrath from us? **9.** For it is also said, 'If you do not turn, he will whet his sword and bend his bow and prepare it. He has prepared therewith instruments of death'[7]. **10.** Moreover it is said, 'The utterance is full of anger, and the anger of his wrath shall devour like fire'[8]. But we have not remembered these things and we have not turned to depart

[Fragment 20] *TO MARY, MOTHER OF JOHN, AND TALOU*

I. **1.** to the place of all suffering, the place of weeping and gnashing of teeth[1] because we have forsaken his words and commandments, which he enjoined upon us with weeping and groaning and great sufferings. **2.** But we, instead of having been to him a consolation there and a satisfaction before God by having walked in propriety and good order[2], we were disdainful, having changed our likeness into another likeness, and we have corrupted

[1a] Jer. 5. 3. [2] Cf. Ps. 36. 27. [3] Jer. 5. 22. [4] Lev. 26. 21. [5] Lev. 26. 19. [6] Lev. 26. 23-24. [7] Ps. 7. 13-14. [8] Is. 30. 27.

[1] Cf. Mt. 8. 12 etc. [2] Cf. I Cor. 14. 40.

our way before God, walking in wickedness, hatred, strife, theft, lying, pride, pollutions, and abominations, that the word which is written may upbraid us, 'She did not forsake the fornication which she committed in Egypt'[3], which means the sins which we have done in the world we have the more perfected still in the holy places of God. **3.** I was not speaking of all the sisters * who fear God and keep his commandments, but rather woe to us who transgress the commandments of our fathers. **4.** Therefore I say to you especially, Mary, mother of John, and Talou, mother of Macarius, and also their foolish daughters and the ignorant who have no salt[4] : if you will not get you understanding and be still and cease from this fashion of needlessly disturbing the place, running up on to the walls and to the gate crying out, 'Indeed, indeed, we shall not stay in this convent which is full of iniquity', or, 'Our case has not been judged'. **5.** Who ill-treats you, except you yourselves? You do violence to the truth of God by your pride and your boastfulness and your scorn and your baseless contempt for your fathers, though they have done you no evil. Even as Talou swore, 'By him who founded this convent[5], I will not stay'.

* p. 55

II. **1.** Ignorant and foolish ones who have no oil in their vessels[6], which means there is no understanding in you neither knowledge nor fear of God, but you are like the horses and the mules which have no wisdom[7]; they leap and kick each other. **2.** So also do you; you quarrel and fight against your fathers with eyes unashamed and with your presumption and hatred, because you are not perfect in the love of God, and the fear of Christ is not before your eyes[8]. **3.** If the community of God is full of iniquity as you have said with your mouth which is full of destruction and offence, then it is you who introduced it there; as it is written, 'But it is you who wrong and rob, not only your sisters[9] but even your fathers also'. **4.** For indeed we have never heard that convents treat men ill, but rather it is the foolish who trouble the convents of God with contention, and strife, and hatred, and evil-

[3] Ez. 23. 8. [4] Cf. Mk. 9. 50, Col. 4. 6. [5] The founder of the White Monastery was Pgol, cf. J. LEIPOLDT, *Schenute von Atripe,* Texte und Untersuchungen 25, 1, N.F. 10, 1, Leipzig, 1903, p. 37. [6] Cf. Mt. 25. 1 ff. [7] Cf. Ps. 31. 9. [8] Cf. Ps. 13. 3, Rom. 3. 18, Ps. 35. 2. [9] Cf. I Cor. 6. 8.

speaking, and all the other wickednesses. **5.** Therefore I promise you in the presence of God and his Christ : if you do not turn * p. 56 away from * such things and go into your house and be quiet sensibly, I shall make your heart sorrowful and I shall cause there to be done to you that which you would not. **6.** Or how, forsooth, shall your words be listened to in the world outside, or those of the world know your doings inside your dwelling? Can it be that such things are profitable to you? It is you who know. **7.** Shall you not therefore put away from you this ignorance and foolishness? How long are we to be in this state, or in these evils, not having purified ourselves so as to follow the Lord our God, the Christ?

III. **1.** Truly, I am grieved with you that you destroy your soul, which the whole world is not worth [10], for the sake of things which yield you no profit but only condemnation and loss. **2.** So let us have mercy upon ourselves. Do not make us bring twofold troubles down upon our head. We shall be past repentance on the day of our visitation and shall find naught to help us there; especially as it was also told us and we did not listen. **3.** And you all, O sisters, fear God and remove yourselves from everything that he hates, and do that which is pleasing to God, as it is written, 'Work out your salvation in fear and trembling' [11], and be subject to your fathers in the fear of Christ, without murmuring and evil thought [12]. **4.** But I tell you that if you do not recognise of what sort you are, and remove, each of you, herself from these evil works, if God so decree, I shall come to you and we shall do to you as God shall ordain, and your heart shall be exceedingly troubled. **5.** 'And I am afraid', as the apostle said, 'lest by any means I should come to you and find you not as I wish, and you should find me not as you wish me; lest by any means there should be strifes, jealousies, wraths, provocations, evil-speakings, whisperings, vanities, and disturbances [13]. I also wrote these things in great grief and much sorrow, lest I should come and have sorrow from them * p. 57 who ought to cause me to rejoice over them' [14]. **6.** For up to * now we have not yet seen any firm conviction. For a brother or brethren who go to law with each other, these are unbelievers [15].

[10] Cf. Mt. 16. 26, Mk. 8. 36, Heb. 11. 38. [11] Phil. 2. 12. [12] Cf. Phil. 2. 14.
[13] II Cor. 12. 20. [14] Cf. II Cor. 2. 3. [15] Cf. I Cor. 6. 6.

IV. **1.** Nevertheless, here are our fathers and our brethren; we have sent them that they should listen, to your words and your works and inform us. Beware, however, do not stop without telling them everything, and also tell them whence or through what [16] these fights and quarrels arose among you. Do you not thus bring yourselves into contempt and bring shame upon those that have (it) not? **2.** And you Mary, mother of John, and Talou, mother of Macarius, and their daughters too, if you have anything to say, do not stop without saying it. **3.** Do not find fault or grumble without cause. And do not stir up the community of God by offensive speech so that our heart is exceedingly grieved because of you, for it is also written, 'He who will offend one of these little ones who believe in me, it is better for him that a millstone should be tied to his neck and he be sunk in the depth of the sea [17], rather than that he should offend one of these little ones who believe in me' [18]. **4.** Else you must needs offend many thus through the things which you have done and said against your fathers, even smiting them; perhaps you will even take unto yourselves staves and strike with them, foolish ones who are not wise. **5.** Or are swords and spears worse than the quarrelsome and scornful tongue? For it is written, 'The teeth of the sons of men are weapons and arrows, and their tongue is a sharp sword' [19]. **6.** Therefore guard us from every evil thing, lest God be angry with us and turn his face from us, and lest all the curses which our father spoke come upon us and make his heart sad concerning us in the place where he is. **7.** But let us all be zealous together that God and his Christ may rejoice over us, and that the heart of our fathers may be at rest; that our heart too may be at rest, not only in this place but in the place to which we shall go; the place where there is rejoicing over the good and grief over the wicked.

[Fragment 21]

TO NUNS WHO ARE DISRUPTING THE COMMUNITY

* Apa Besa. * p. 58

I. **1.** Whereas we have heard that there are some who make disturbances among you and pointless contentions from which God

16 Or : 'whom'. 17 Mt. 18. 6. 18 Cf. Lk. 17. 2. 19 Ps. 56. 5.

has no gain, I therefore promise you all in the sight of God and Christ Jesus, our Lord : if you will not fear God and put away from you these follies and this hardness of heart and obey your fathers and superiors who take care of you, I will cause you to go round seeking [1] each one of you, and you will not know what shall befall them. **2.** Will you not fear the Lord? Or will you not be in awe before him? [2] Did each one of you come to this convent to fight, or quarrel, or contradict, or grumble, or be disobedient, or steal, or lie, or provoke the word of the Lord to anger? **3.** Did we not all come to repent of our wickednesses, which we did in the sight of the Lord Jesus, and to take care that we should not sin yet again before him and he be very angry with us? **4.** Will you be able to bear the wrath of man that you would bear the wrath of the Lord? I think that such things as you do are profitless to you. **5.** You shall neither benefit by them, nor are we gathered together in this convent to do things unfitting, in particular pollution, theft, lying, contention, strife, envy, and hatred. For because of these things comes the wrath of God upon the sons of unbelief [3] who are the lovers of evil.

II. **1.** For this reason therefore, sisters, do not let us love the evil lest we perish, but let us open our eyes and look at the things that are upright [4] lest by any means we regret it at our end, and afterwards grieve over ourselves with weeping, and sorrow, and groaning, saying, 'Why did I not want them to teach me, and my heart turn away from reproofs? [5] **2.** Why did I not listen to the voice of him who teaches me, and did not incline my ear to him who instructs me?' [6] For indeed the son who forsakes instruction
* p. 59 will fall upon evils and will meditate iniquitous words [7]. **3.** * Now therefore, let us remove ourselves from wickedness. We shall not be afraid and no trembling will come nigh unto us. **4.** If you do not remove yourselves from the things which God hates, you will not know the time when I shall come to you and do to each one of you according to her deserts; according to the word which the apostle spoke, 'Lest by any means I should come to you and find you not

[1] Possibly a reference to the nuns' fate after a threatened expulsion from the convent. [2] Cf. Jer. 5. 22. [3] Eph. 5. 6. [4] Cf. Prov. 4. 25. [5] Prov. 5. 12. [6] Cf. Prov. 5. 13. [7] Cf. Prov. 19. 24.

as I wish, and you should find me also not as you wish me; lest by any means there should be strifes, jealousies, wraths, provocations, evil-speakings, whisperings, vanities, and disturbances'[8]. **5.** Therefore he said sharply, 'If I come again I shall not spare'[9]. Is there no balm in Gilead or is there no physician there? Why did the healing of the daughter of my people not come up? [10] **6.** This means, do we lack teaching from our fathers or that they instruct us from the scriptures and the gospels of our Lord Jesus Christ? Why did the healing of the trespasses not come up? Or why did we not remove ourselves from the wickednesses? **7.** Why do we draw down upon ourselves the curse of the scriptures and the wrath of God because of our hardening of heart and our presumptuousness?

III. **1.** Now therefore, sisters, let us forsake the works of darkness and put upon us the armour of light[11]. For you know the works of darkness, what they are; and what the works of light are. **2.** For everyone who does good is of God but he who does evil is of the devil[12] and does not know God. Let us then fear lest it be said threateningly to us, 'Is not the Lord in Zion or is there no king there? Why did you provoke me to anger with your carved images and these strange vanities?'[13] **3.** But let it rather be said of us with confidence, 'Are they not my people, my children? They will not deal treacherously'[14]. **4.** Now therefore, O people, whose heart is far astray from righteousness, pay heed to teaching and prepare your ears for the words of knowledge[15]. **5.** If it is said, 'If the righteous will scarcely be saved, then where will the ungodly and the sinner appear'[16], then how * shall we escape if we neglect this great principle and this so great salvation[17] into which we foolish and ignorant ones have entered? For it is said, 'The foolish and the ignorant shall perish together'[18]. **6.** But if it is also said, 'God resists the proud but gives grace to the humble'[19], then why do we draw down upon ourselves the destruction of our soul? We do not perceive our condemnation because of our boastfulness and the hardening of our heart. **7.** Solomon also says, 'A wise son obeys his father but a disobedient son is in perdition'[20]. But we bring

* p. 60

8 II Cor. 12. 20. 9 II Cor. 13. 2. 10 Jer. 8. 22. 11 Rom. 13. 12. 12 Cf. I Jn. 3. 8. 13 Cf. Jer. 8. 19. 14 Is. 63. 8. 15 Cf. Prov. 23. 12. 16 I Pet. 4. 18. 17 Cf. Heb. 2. 3. 18 Ps. 48. 11. 19 Prov. 3. 34, I Pet. 5. 5, Jam. 4. 6. 20 Prov. 13. 1.

our own perdition upon us. Because of our disobedience we were not ashamed so as to choose for ourselves life rather than death, and we were not wise to acquire for ourselves guidance [21].

[Fragment 22] *TO MARY, SISTER OF MATAI*

By the same.

I. **1.** But you Mary, sister of Matai, will you not put away from you this hardness of heart and this pride which will not profit you, and will you not hear that the hard of heart will be filled with his own ways [1]; **2.** and again that the hard of heart will meet with no good [2]; and again that the foolish man digs for himself evils and gathers up a fire on his lips? [3] **3.** Therefore I say unto you, ignorant one, if you will not put away from you this shamelessness, I shall cause your heart to be grieved. **4.** Is it a small thing to you to fight against men? And how can you fight against the Lord with your struggle and your strife and your disobedience, driving away from you the mercy of God, and dishonouring your own soul by your contempt and ranting [4] at your fathers who take care of you at all times and who are in travail for your souls, that God may give them repentance unto the knowledge of the truth, that you may recover yourselves from the snares of the devil? [5] **5.** And we therefore did not understand. If you had had any understanding, would you have cried out among the sisters, 'Indeed, indeed, I shall go where my children are', in your stiff-neckedness
* p. 61 and your boastfulness, and, 'I am not going * to the gate to receive punishment'? **6.** And have you not thus disobeyed our injunction? Was it not we that said, let them go to the gate and receive punishment? Did we not do it for your profit, so that God may forgive you and receive your prayer to himself, because we are wretched and do not know how we are coming into the hands of God? **7.** For if you had not been foolish, would you have said, 'I shall go where my children are'? But where are your children? For if they had not done wickedness would they go to perdition?

21 Cf. Prov. 1. 5.

1 Prov. 14. 14. 2 Prov. 17. 20. 3 Prov. 16. 27. 4 Lit. : 'roaring', 'neighing'. 5 Cf. II Tim. 2. 25-26.

You too want to go to perdition where those are, because the fear of God is far from you and you do not take thought for your end. **8.** Do you not thus despise the grace of God and spurn the grace which he wrought, not for you alone but for all of us, having brought us out of the iron furnace[6] which is the world, having redeemed us from out of the midst of perdition? **9.** And he brought us into honour of which we are not worthy, so that the word which is written may say to me and to you, 'He who shall recompense evil for good, evil will not stir from his house'[7].

II. **1.** Do you not hear the Lord God speaking to the children of Israel, blaming them and scorning them and upbraiding them, 'You are a stiff-necked people, beware lest I bring another calamity upon you to wipe you out'?[8] The children of Israel heard this hard saying and grieved. **2.** But we hear of our shame and our condemnation because of our hardness of heart and our boastfulness — that which is called pestilence — and we do not perceive nor do we repent of our wickednesses, lest the Lord Jesus be angry with us and cast us together with those who work lawlessness[9]. **3.** Or do we not hear, when Miriam[10] had spoken and murmured against Moses, what was said to her from the Lord? — namely that, 'If her father had spit in her face, should she not be ashamed for seven days? Let her be separate outside the camp for seven days'[11], for she had even become leprous. **4.** So the holy man Moses said to them in his benevolence, 'Give heed to the matter of leprosy'[12], which is evil-speaking. But the leprosy of our wickednesses is before us at all times and we are upbraided * by the Lord Jesus every day * p. 62
and we are not ashamed and our heart does not blame us so as to make us turn away from our evil works and do good. **5.** Therefore I tell you that if you will not go and receive punishment as it was told you, I think that the wrath of God will proceed to work upon you strangely[13], and afterwards you will be grieved at your own self. For you are a perverse woman, bringing upon you your own perdition by your mouth, and drawing down upon yourself the curse of God. **6.** But here is our father, Apa Isaac; we have sent him to

[6] Cf. Deut. 4. 20, III Kg. 8. 51, Jer. 11. 4. [7] Prov. 17. 13. [8] Ex. 33. 5.
[9] Cf. Ps. 124. 5. [10] Cf. Num. 12. 1 ff. [11] Num. 12. 14. [12] Deut. 24. 8.
[13] Cf. Is. 28. 21.

you and the other elders that they may examine your words. And do not hide anything from him. Let him return to us from you with satisfaction [14].

[Fragment 23] *ON THEFT AND DECEITFUL BEHAVIOUR*

I. **1.** But I speak to you all, you ignorant people and false brethren who have not put the fear of God before them, but still persist in your thefts and your deceptions and your lies which are full of every evil, and you were not ashamed so as to remove yourselves from these ungodlinesses which you do, and feared not God nor respected man [1]. **2.** Therefore you are cursed and your judgement and your condemnation are upon you, because you have been taught many times and you did not pay heed. And even though your ears were open you did not hear. **3.** Your heart was hard and crass, for you had no understanding, and you did not receive the teaching and the commandments which our fathers enjoined upon us, according to that which was said, 'For the heart of this people was hardened and they were slow to hear with their ears, and they shut their eyes lest they might see with their eyes and hear with their ears and turn and I may heal them' [2], or have mercy upon them. **4.** O, the hope of those who do such impious deeds is cursed, * p. 63 * because they have despised the name of God by their evil works and they have brought shame upon those that have (it) not, having also despised the name of our blessed fathers in their ignorance because of their thefts and lies and deceptions. **5.** And, having gone away, they went into vineyards that they might spoil and steal without permission and without telling anyone that they would go, drawing the curse of God down upon themselves because of their thoughtlessness and the hardness of their heart. **6.** They have not thought nor considered that the things they do are not small

14 Probably the end of a letter, cf. P. VAN CAUWENBERGH, *Étude sur les moines d'Égypte depuis le Concile de Chalcédoine (451) jusqu'à l'invasion arabe (640)*, Paris, 1914, p. 5, though this is not indicated in the MS., and W. E. Crum (*Catalogue of the Coptic Manuscripts in the Collection of the John Rylands Library Manchester*, Manchester, 1909, p. 27) does not think that the letter ends here.

1 Cf. Lk. 18. 2. 2 Cf, Is. 6. 10, Mt. 13. 15.

sins, in that they let others benefit by their sins, but they destroy their own soul unknowingly, stealing and spoiling, robbing on this side and that, pilfering even jars of wine and grapes, so that those who see them blaspheme against God and say, 'Are these monks?' Or, 'Are these the people of Apa Shenoute?' [3] And, 'Shall then not anybody be? What do we do more than they?'

II. **1.** It has been said, 'Let them see your good works and glorify your Father which is in heaven' [4]. But you despised him until they despised the name of our fathers because of your evil works. **2.** Instead of saying 'Behold a people wise and of understanding' or 'Behold a seed blessed by God', they rather despised the name of our holy monastery. O you concerning whom these things are said, you are responsible because you have not feared Christ nor respected man [5]. **3.** Therefore woe to you, because a judge who neither feared God nor respected man, gave judgement for a widow that she should not be coming to him so often and troubling him [6]. **4.** But you were not ashamed nor did you notice when you were being reproached and frequently instructed to have pity upon yourselves and cease from your wickednesses and learn to do good [7] before you become like a flower that perishes, before the wrath of the Lord comes upon you, and before your soul is plucked out from within you and you break your spirit with tears down in hell, with none to hear you and no one to have pity on you. **5.** When * you were called, * p. 64
you did not hear. And words were spread abroad : you paid no heed. But you rejected the counsels of the Lord in your presumptuousness and you disobeyed his upbraidings. **6.** Therefore he will also mock at your perdition and he will deride you when perdition comes upon you [8] at the time of your visitation, and when tribulation comes to you and you are in straits [9] down in hell in the time of your need. **7.** 'For I called you', he says, 'you did not hear me, I spoke and you heeded not, you did evil in my sight and you chose the things which I do not wish'.

III. **1.** Therefore he says, 'Behold they who are servants of mine shall eat, but you will be hungry. Behold they who are servants of

[3] Besa's predecessor as abbot of the White Monastery. [4] Cf. Mt. 5. 16. [5] Cf. Lk. 18. 2. [6] Cf. Lk. 18. 2 ff. [7] Cf. Is. 1. 16-17. [8] Cf. Prov. 1. 24-26. [9] Prov. 1. 27. — Cf. p. 12, n. 16.

mine shall drink, but you will be thirsty. Behold they who are servants of mine shall rejoice, but you will be ashamed. Behold they who are servants of mine shall exult with joy, but you will cry for the sorrow of your heart and you will cry out because of the destruction of your spirit. **2.** For you have renounced the name of your Lord which is satisfaction for my chosen ones, but the Lord will kill you'[10], because you persist in your wickednesses and your thefts, stealing each other's garments in your impudence and your shamelessness. **3.** Unclean ones, who are notorious in your lawlessnesses and your obstinate sins! And you steal each other's things[11], even down to the very linen clothes[12] you carry off. **4.** Did people come in to us and take them? (No,) but there are thieves in the midst of us, the community, seizing whatever they can find, drawing the curse of God upon them, even boasting with their mouths — which ought to shut up — and their deceitful, bragging tongues, saying, 'They did not catch us in anything nor did they know concerning us of the things which we do'[13]. **5.** They did not know that God would divide them in their midst so that everyone might see them, nor did they say with their mouths which are full of cursing and bitterness[14], 'The wrath of the Lord will burn those men until he wipes them out of his communities'; **6.** as it is written, 'Behold an earthquake comes from the Lord and
* p. 65 wrath unto turmoil, whirling and coming * down upon the godless. The wrath of the Lord will not turn to cease there, until he performs and completes the desire of his heart'[15] upon the godless who do impious deeds, and thefts, and lies, and deceits. **7.** 'The heaven was fearful about this matter and the earth trembled greatly', says the Lord[16]. 'They have forsaken me, the fountain of living water', which is the truth, 'they have dug for themselves broken cisterns'[17], which are thieving and falsehood and deceit.

IV. **1.** The faithful or the honest man is not he who was not caught in his evils by men, but the truly faithful and honest man is he who was not seized or caught by God. For not he who shall commend himself is the elect, but whom God shall commend[18].

[10] Is. 65. 12-15. [11] Lit.: 'tool', 'weapon'. [12] Lit.: 'linen'. [13] Cf. Is. 29. 15. [14] Cf. Ps. 9. 28, Rom. 3. 14. [15] Jer. 23. 19-20. [16] Jer. 2. 12. [17] Jer. 2. 13. [18] II Cor. 10. 18.

2. For on this it has been said, 'The foolish and the ignorant shall perish together' [19], and again it is said, 'Man being in honour did not understand, he was likened to ignorant beasts, he resembled them' [20]. **3.** This is your own way. You have despised the grace of God in your boastfulness and your pride, O you hard of heart and uncircumcised in heart and ears too! [21] **4.** For you are the seed of those about whom it was said, 'You always resist the Holy Spirit like your fathers' [22] which are the devil and his demons. **5.** This is your own way, you being disobedient to the commandments of the Lord in your contempt and the hardness of your ignorant heart. **6.** Woe to you, you have multiplied the things of death by your contempt and your indifference. Foolish and ignorant ones, how shall you escape the judgement of Gehenna! **7.** Woe to you, because you have not understood neither have you learned wisdom, walking in the darkness of your disobedience because your ignorant hearts were darkened [23] from thieving and deceit. **8.** Woe to you, what shall you do on the day of visitation? Your affliction is coming from afar and to whom will you flee to help you [24], because you have despised the words of the Lord and brought his commandments to naught? **9.** So also the Lord will bring you to naught and he will plunge you into the fiery furnace in hell. Unclean ones, who are notorious * in lawlessnesses! For the ways wherein you walk are * p. 66
crooked [25] and you have been unable to go through the straight [26].

V. **1.** It has been said, 'Sow for yourselves unto righteousness and reap a fruit of life' [27], but you sowed iniquity and reaped lawlessness. **2.** Thus again it has been said, 'Sow wheat and reap thorns. Their lots', it was said, 'shall not profit them' [28], which means their prayers and their fastings and their recitations shall not profit them because of their lawlessnesses by which they have worked iniquity. **3.** For they waited for light, darkness befell them; they awaited light, yet they walked in darkness. They will grope for the wall like a blind man and they will feel as do those who have no eyes, and they will fall at noonday like those at midnight [29], which means you have sinned like those who never

19 Ps. 48. 11. 20 Ps. 48. 13, Ps. 48. 21. 21 Cf. Acts 7. 51. 22 Acts 7. 51.
23 Cf. Rom. 1. 21. 24 Is. 10. 3. 25 Cf. Is. 59. 8. 26 Cf. Is. 59. 14.
27 Hos. 10. 12. 28 Jer. 12. 13. 29 Is. 59, 9-10.

knew scripture and were entirely untaught. **4.** For your works are works of lawlessness and their feet run to evil, they hasten to shed blood. And your thoughts are foolish thoughts [30], you think of thieving and lying and every evil. **5.** So therefore the wind will take you [31], which is the anger of the wrath of God, so that you will not find for yourselves the way of rest. Because you have provoked God to anger, he has turned to you in enmity [32]. **6.** But you, brethren, who fear God, the Lord will bless you and save you from all these curses and he will guard you from every evil and from one who speaks nothing of truth, which is the devil [33]. **7.** But the Lord Jesus will save you into his kingdom which is in heaven [34] and he will keep your spirit sound and your soul and your body without sin at the advent of our Lord Jesus Christ [35].

VI. **1.** But you, brethren, were not in darkness that the day should overtake you as a thief; for you are all sons of the light and sons of the day; you are not of the night nor of the darkness. **2.** So then let us not sleep as do the rest, but let us watch and be sober. For those who sleep sleep in the night, and those who are
* p. 67 drunk are drunk in the night. * But we are of the day. Let us be sober, having put upon us the breastplate of faith and love, and the helmet of the hope of salvation. For God did not appoint us unto wrath but unto a preservation [36] of salvation through our Lord Jesus, he who died for us in order that, whether we watch or sleep, we may live with him [37]. **3.** Now therefore, brethren, let us not be like the false brethren in our midst who walk in deceit, but work out your salvation in fear and trembling [38] that the Lord Jesus may guard you in all your works. **4.** For it is God who works in you the will and the fulfilment of the will. Do all things without murmuring and disputing, that you may become sinless and innocent, children of God, holy, in the midst of the crooked and perverse generation among whom you are manifested even as the enlighteners in the world, persisting in the word of life for a glorying unto me on the day of Christ [39]. **5.** So then if

30 Cf. Is. 59. 6-7. 31 Cf. Is. 64. 6. 32 Cf. Is. 63. 10. 33 Cf. Jn. 8. 44. 34 Cf. II Tim. 4 18. 35 I Thes. 5. 23. 36 Lit. : 'keeping alive', 'saving'. The Greek N.T. here has περιποίησις which in this context means : 'acquisition', 'obtaining'. 37 I Thes. 5. 4-10. 38 Phil. 2. 12. 39 Phil. 2. 13-16.

we keep the commandments of our fathers, they will pride themselves on us before the Lord, saying, 'Are these not my children? They will not deal treacherously'[40]. **6.** And again, 'Behold, we and the children you gave us[41]; we have laboured for them for the sake of your name'. **7.** The Lord will then give us means to escape all the snares of the adversary and be rich in good works[42] before we come into the judgement of God, and to escape the punishments prepared for the sinners who persist in their evils.

[Fragment 24] *ON STEALING FROM THE SICK*

By the same.

I. **1.** It is right for you and good for your soul, wretched ones, to learn whence you are, and give glory to the Lord your God before the darkness comes and your feet stumble upon the dark mountains. You will look for light, a shadow of death is there; and they shall be put in darkness. **2.** But if you do not hear, your soul will weep secretly confronted with your shame and your eyes will shed tears[1] with no one to wipe * your tears from your eyes[2]. * p. 68
3. For you were called and you did not hear, you were spoken to and heeded not, you did evil in the sight of the Lord and chose the things he did not wish[3]. **4.** How long then will we draw down upon us the word which is written, 'The ungodly passed over the landmark'[4], because you steal, you lie, you are disobedient, you work iniquity, you act lawlessly, you violate the commandments of Christ, you destroy your body, you sin in everything, as it was said, 'The way of the daughter of my people is not towards uprightness nor towards purity'[5], and again, 'This is your wickedness, for it is bitter, because it reached to your heart'[6]. **5.** Moreover it was said, in censuring the untaught and foolish ones amongst us who have not learned wisdom but walked in darkness, 'Is there no balm in Gilead or is there no physician there? Why did the healing of the daughter of my people not come up?'[7] which means, is there no scripture among us or have we not been taught in the law of the

40 Cf. Is. 63. 8. 41 Cf. Is. 8. 18, Heb. 2. 13. 42 Cf. I Tim. 6. 18.
1 Jer. 13. 16-17. 2 Cf. perhaps Rev. 7. 17. 3 Cf. Is. 65. 12, Is. 66. 4.
4 Job 24. 2. 5 Jer. 4. 11. 6 Jer. 4. 18. 7 Jer. 8. 22.

Lord namely, 'Cease from your wickednesses, learn to do good'?[8] **6.** Yet we were not afraid and did not realise that we should depart from our inciting of God to wrath by our evil deeds, but we chose to bring upon us the word which is written, 'Because of your hardness and your impenitent heart, you treasure up for yourself wrath in the day of wrath and the revelation of the just judgement of God, who will render to every man according to his works'[9].

II. **1.** For were we not told or do we lack teaching that we should guard ourselves from evil, in accordance with the saying, 'He who does not tell his son at the outset to guard himself from evil will perish suddenly'?[10] **2.** And we did not hearken so that the evil increased among us and God was angry with us, as it was said, 'They were disobedient, they have provoked his holy spirit to anger and the Lord has turned to them in enmity'[11]. **3.** Woe to us for we * p. 69 have sinned! That is why our heart was grieved[12]. * Our ignorance will teach us and our wickedness will upbraid us. Know therefore and understand that it is bitter for us to forsake the commandments of God[13] and the laws of our fathers. **4.** For thus it was said, 'But this people has got a disobedient and unbelieving heart : they turned away and departed; they did not say in their heart, "Let us fear the Lord who gives us the former and the latter rain" '[14], that is to say the blessing of God which is upon us because of our fathers. **5.** And again, 'Woe to me my soul, because the godfearing has perished from the earth and the upright among men is not'[15]. **6.** But even down to the barest necessity which you are given for the sick you acted wickedly to your own selves — you stole it from each other. Even this great wickedness is on your heads, for we have never heard of such a transgression. **7.** Therefore they who do these things are cursed all the more before God and men, for you also were very ungodly. Thus your sin is double upon you, because these are not little sins that you do.

III. **1.** O truly wicked ones, who do great wickednesses over which the heaven and the earth shall be troubled and fearful![16]

8 Is. 1. 16-17. 9 Rom. 2. 5-6. 10 Prov. 24. 22. — This clause, though in the Sah. (W. H. WORRELL, *The Proverbs of Solomon in Sahidic Coptic*, Chicago, 1931), is not in the LXX. 11 Is. 63. 10. 12 Lam. 5. 16-17. 13 Cf. Jer. 2. 19. 14 Jer. 5. 23-24. 15 Mic. 7. 1-2. 16 Cf. Jer. 2. 12.

2. The righteous and the brethren who love Christ truly and who tremble at his name shall see and be afraid and say, 'Behold, men who did not make God their helper but set their hope upon their vanity and their lying delusions'[17]. **3.** The people who say, 'No one shall know concerning us of the things which we do stealthily'[18], woe to them, and what will they do on the day when everyone's iniquities shall be revealed? **4.** For it has been said, 'He who shares with a thief — which is the devil — hates his own soul. But if an oath is sworn', it has been said, 'and they do not reveal it, they shall fall and be ashamed because they feared men; but blessed is he who fears God'[19]. **5.** But on this it has been said, 'Death will befall the ignorant[20], uncleannesses will defile a pestilent man on an evil and troublous day until he perishes'[21]. Woe to you who do these and other detestable and wholly deceitful things by stealth! **6.** O you are cursed in all your works because * you have put your hand to these lawless deeds, having despised the name of God in your deceptions. And you have brought shame on those that have (it) not. **7.** Therefore God, for his part, and his Christ will destroy you and hand you over to all shame and every affliction and the fire that is not quenched and the worm that never dies[22] down in hell. **8.** For out of great affliction and much grief[23] I say these things, because we never either heard or saw such an iniquitous thing, that men stole their neighbours' necessities so that the curse should be doubled upon them. * p. 70

IV. **1.** Indeed every theft is evil and cursed in the sight of our Lord Jesus, but this is still more evil in the sight of God and men. And it is more evil than any transgression and shamelessness. It even leads on to murder. **2.** For if a man take the thing needful to a sick man, he is as good as that man's murderer. Like those who gave the Lord in his thirst vinegar to drink[24], so are they for their part now, for they steal the thing needful to their sick brethren **3.** This great curse and this great wrath is upon those who do such things. So they are greatly cursed, and all the people shall say, 'It shall be so'[25]. **4.** And even as it was said, 'Cursed

17 Cf. Ps. 51. 9 and Ps. 39. 5. 18 Cf. Is. 29. 15. 19 Prov. 29. 24-25. 20 Prov. 24. 8. 21 Prov. 24. 9-10. 22 Cf. Is. 66. 24, Mk. 9. 48. 23 Cf. II Cor. 2. 4. 24 Cf. Mt. 27. 48 and parallels. 25 Deut. 27. 15 etc.

be he who shall remove his neighbour's landmarks and all the people shall say, "It shall be so" '[26], so shall he come to be cursed who has stolen or shall steal from the shares of his neighbours, whether their necessities, or their money, or their clothing, or their cloak, or anything which is theirs, for none lack anything that they need, but they sin against themselves and draw the curse of God upon themselves. **5.** And those who shall actually raise their hand against their fathers, who teach them, with a stick or a blow[27], they shall be cursed in the sight of God and men, and shall be called in the scriptural phrase 'stumbling-blocks'[28] which are in the way, as it is written, 'Take these stumbling-blocks out of they way of my people'[29]. **6.** And those who shall quarrel with them ever in their hardness of heart and their boastfulness and their shamelessness, they shall be called 'Men who fight against * p. 71 God and his Christ in their stiff-neckedness and * their pride', **7.** so that God for his part will contend against them, and cast them together with those who work lawlessness[30], as it is written, 'He who despises his father and his mother thinking, "I do not sin", is an associate of an ungodly man'[31].

V. **1.** Again it is said, 'The son who despises his father and forsakes his mother shall be under reproach and be ashamed'[32] And again, 'The light of him who reviles his father and his mother shall go out, the pupils of his eyes shall see darkness'[33]. **2.** Thus again it was said, 'God resists the proud but gives grace to the humble'[34]. And again, 'You have humbled the proud like a thing slain', which means the devil and all those who do his works. **3.** And, 'You have scattered your enemies with the arm of your strength'[35], which means the sinners who do wickedness before him. **4.** And on this it has been said, 'They shall be portions for foxes'[36], which are the demons who beguile them and work in them every lawlessness. **5.** As it was said of Babylon at that time, 'We healed her but she was not healed; let us abandon her and go, because her judgement reached up to heaven, it mounted aloft

26 Deut. 27. 17. 27 Meaning doubtful, cf. CRUM, *Dictionary*, p. 431 b. 28 Cf. Is. 57. 14. 29 Is. 57. 14. 30 Cf. Ps. 124. 5. 31 Prov. 28. 24. 32 Prov. 19. 23. 33 Prov. 20. 10. 34 Prov. 3. 34, I Pet. 5. 5, Jam. 4. 6. 35 Ps. 88. 11. 36 Ps. 62. 11.

to the stars' [37], so shall the angels of God and those who teach you forsake you, saying, 'We taught them but they were not taught; let us depart from them, because their judgement reached unto God and his Christ, who will judge each one according to his works' [38]. **6.** For it is he who knows those who do wickedness in secret, and also he does not forget those who do good before him and those who tremble at his name. **7.** Therefore as the Lord said, 'Unless the grain of wheat falls upon the earth and dies it remains alone, but if it die it bears much fruit' [39]. **8.** Thus also unless a man mortifies his body, he shall be without avail in his works, but if he mortify it he shall bear much fruit in good works, as it is written, 'He who died in the flesh ceased from sin so as to be no longer in the lusts of men, but rather spend the rest of the days of his life according to the will of God' [40].

[Fragment 25] *TO THIEVING NUNS*

I. **1.** * O, yours is the responsibility, you who give opportunity * p. 72
to Satan to come in and pollute the holy convents of God! And you defile his temple which is you yourselves [1]. You have not called to mind the apostle's assertion, 'He who defiles the temple of God, him will God destroy' [2]. **2.** Also you have not remembered all the curses which our father pronounced when giving us all into the hand of God saying [3], 'He is cursed who shall defile his body in any way, or shall steal anything' — including a cord or strap [3a], more especially garments, cloaks, cowls, or even the least thing to eat, either from the things for the service of God or from the shares of their neighbours. **3.** I was thinking indeed of coming to you with a mind at rest, but the grief for those who have provoked God to anger and grieved his Holy Spirit [4] prevented our gladness. **4.** I know indeed what I deserve is every grief but, if God and our Lord Jesus desire it, I am coming to you in wrath to do all the things that are in my heart to these

37 Cf. Jer. 28. 9. 38 Cf. I Pet. 1. 17. 39 Jn. 12. 24. 40 I Pet. 4. 1-2.

1 Cf. I Cor. 3. 16-17. 2 I Cor. 3. 17. 3 Perhaps a reference to the vow introduced by Shenoute, cf. J. Leipoldt, *Sinuthii archimandritae vita et opera omnia*, Paris, CSCO, 42/Copt.2 (1908), p. 20, and 73/Copt.5 (1913), p. 40. 3a Cf. Gen. 14. 23. 4 Cf. Eph. 4. 30.

ignorant persons and foolish virgins who have no oil in their vessels [5]; **5.** seeing that you turn back again to [6] these provocations of God and fall upon the sword of the evil one who corrupted all the world in his sins and his lawlessness, because you have loved defilement rather than purity, and have chosen for yourselves death rather than life [7]. **6.** For you have incited him who made you and nourished you, God, the Eternal, to wrath and you have also grieved her who nursed you, Jerusalem [8], that is to say the community. And you fell at noonday like those at midnight [9], as it is written, 'The virgin of Israel stumbled, she fell, she shall no more rise' [10]. **7.** 'For those who sleep', it is said, 'sleep in the night and those who are drunk are drunk in the night' [11]. But * p. 73 you were drunk at noonday like * those about whom it was said, 'They are drunk without wine' [12]. And you slept at noonday like those who sleep in the night, because you forsook the fear of God and loved the darkness rather than the light [13], and also reckoned the bitter sweet and the sweet bitter [14].

II. **1.** So woe to you, wicked ones, because you have not called to mind all the trouble which our father took with you all, but have forsaken his teachings of life and the ordinances of your fathers. **2.** Nevertheless, here are the elders and our brethren; they have come to you again because we are living in great distress and much grief, that they may do to each of you according to her deserts. **3.** For you have forsaken the fountain of living water and dug for yourselves broken cisterns [15] and, when your ignorant hearts were darkened and you said, 'We are wise', you became fools, having exchanged the glory of God [16] for unfitting things. **4.** Therefore God has given you up to despicable passions [17], that is to say theft and pollution and every wickedness, for the doers of which things there are all sorts of punishment, not only in this age but in the next [18].

5 Cf. Mt. 25. 1 ff. 6 Crum, wrongly I think, gives : 'turn back from, out of', cf. Crum, *Dictionary*, p. 644 b. 7 Cf. Jer. 8. 3. 8 Cf. Bar. 4. 7-8. 9 Cf. Is. 59. 10. 10 Cf. Amos 5. 2. 11 I Thes. 5. 7. 12 Cf. Is. 29. 9, Is. 51. 21. 13 Cf. Jn. 3. 19. 14 Cf. Is. 5. 20. 15 Cf. Jer. 2. 13. 16 Cf. Rom. 1. 21-23. 17 Cf. Rom. 1. 26. 18 Eph. 1. 21.

[Fragment 26] *ON TRANSGRESSING THE LAWS OF GOD AND THE PRECEPTS OF THE FATHERS*

By the same.

I. **1.** Our teacher and our Lord Jesus Christ, our Saviour, exhorts and teaches us saying, 'Walk as long as you have the light, that the darkness may not overtake you' [1]. **2.** And, 'He who walks in the day does not stumble, because he sees the light of this world. He who walks in the night stumbles because the light is not in it' [2]. **3.** We also, if we walk in the laws of God and the commandments of our fathers, shall not stumble, because the light is in them. For it is said, 'I walked by his light in the darkness' [3]. **4.** If we turn ourselves away from the commandments of God and our fathers' teachings * which they gave us, we shall stumble, since we * p. 74 know not whither we go [4] because the darkness has shut our eyes, and we shall grope like those who have no eyes [5]. **5.** For it is said, 'The good commandment is a lamp, and the law is a light for the way' [6]. And again, 'Your word is the lamp of my feet and the light of my ways' [7]. **6.** And again, 'My spirit shall come early out of the night, it shall come early to you, O God, because your statutes are lights upon the earth' [8]. And again, 'The law of the Lord is holy, converting souls' [9]. Whither does it convert them except from evil to good, from darkness to light? **7.** And again, 'The commandment of the Lord is a light which enlightens the eyes of the young' [10]. And again, 'He who shall keep the commandment shall know no evil thing' [11]. And again, 'He who shall keep the commandment is saved' [12]. **8.** Surely, if we transgress the commandment, we are like him who perished and was broken. For he who lacks these things is blind and sees not, having forgotten the cleansing of his former sins [13].

II. **1.** For truly the mother of us all, which is wisdom, teaches us saying, 'My son, let not evil counsel overtake you which forsakes teaching from its youth and forgets the holy covenant. **2.** For it set its house near death and its path with men near hell. None

1 Jn. 12. 35. 2 Jn. 11. 9-10. 3 Job 29. 3. 4 Cf. Jn. 12. 35. 5 Cf. Is. 59. 10. 6 Prov. 6. 23. 7 Ps. 118. 105. 8 Is. 26. 9. 9 Ps. 18. 8. 10 Ps. 18. 9. 11 Eccles. 8. 5. 12 Cf. Prov. 13. 13. 13 II Pet. 1. 9.

that adheres thereto shall return or attain to the ways of life. But they shall regret, because the years of life shall not affect them. For if they had walked on the good paths, they would have found the ways of the righteous smooth'[14]. **3.** If we pay heed to the teachings of the scriptures strictly and obey them, we shall not stumble nor shall we act scornfully so as to live in all wickedness, but we shall obey him who says, 'Lay hold on the good, abstain from every evil thing'[15], in order that we may have many ways of life. **4.** For it is said, 'He who loves the law surrounds himself with a wall'[16]. And again it is said, 'He gave the law for a help'[17]. * p. 75 **5.** * If a man takes refuge with God and fears him and observes his laws and his commandments, the Lord becomes his helper and preserves him from every evil way and from one who speaks nothing of truth, which is the devil[18], who envies those who wish to live in godliness. **6.** Woe, therefore, to those who forsake the laws of God and neglect the commandments of our fathers which they enjoined upon us. **7.** For it shall rightly be said, 'Woe to them because they turned away from me; misery shall overtake them because they did iniquity against me'[19]. **8.** And to us it shall be said, 'O forsakers of the straight ways, who choose for themselves the ways of darkness, who take pleasure in them that do evil and who rejoice at the wicked, whose ways are twisted and whose paths are so devious[20] that they become remote and estrange themselves from the purpose of the righteous'[21].

III. **1.** So all who transgress the commandments which our fathers laid down for us, and who buy and sell fraudulently, or sell or buy without asking permission, or eat and drink covertly either outside or inside the community against the rules which our fathers laid down for us, unless they have told it previously, shall be cursed with all their works, especially if they eat anything different from what has been allowed to us. **2.** Again we are found despising and forsaking the ordinances and the things which our fathers laid down for us concerning foods of the belly that perish[22], even after it was written for us, 'Because of food do not

14 Prov. 2. 16-20. 15 I Thes. 5. 21-22. 16 Cf. Prov. 28. 4. 17 Is. 8. 20.
18 Cf. Jn. 8. 44. 19 Hos. 7. 13. 20 Prov. 2. 13-15. 21 Cf. Prov. 2. 16.
22 Cf. Jn. 6. 27, I Cor. 6. 13.

destroy the work of God'[23]. **3.** It is not a sin or a fault in us if we ask concerning everything before acting: But, on the other hand, it is lawlessness for us and a great iniquity on our part if we do anything or go anywhere without having first asked permission, or if we eat anything covertly or drink wine without having informed those who take care of us. **4.** And if we do such a thing without asking permission, our blood is on our heads. Moreover those who do these things shall be fettered in their thoughts[24] and they shall be called in the scriptural phrase, 'Portions for foxes'[25], which means demons. **5.** And again the word which is written will speak to us thus, * 'They who turn away from your commandments are cursed'[26], and again, 'You have despised all who are far from your statutes, because their thoughts are iniquity'[27], and again, 'Salvation is far from the sinners because they did not seek after your statutes'[28]. * p. 76

IV. **1.** Therefore, brethren, it is good for us to acquire for ourselves the fear of the Lord and to depart from the things which God hates, that we may find grace on the day of our visitation, since we do not know how we shall meet God and our Lord Jesus. **2.** For it is a very hard thing to meet God. He whom we shall meet is not a man like us, but he is Lord and God, knowing the things we do in the darkness. **3.** For it is said, ' "Shall anyone be able to hide himself in a secret place and I not see him? Do I not fill the heaven and the earth?" says the Lord'[29]. For to turn ourselves from evil is the way of life, and the fear of the Lord is the beginning of wisdom[30]. **4.** Now therefore far be it from us to acquire disrespect and to sin before God lest we regret at our end, but let us pay heed to teaching and incline our ears to the words of knowledge[31], that we may know how we are, lest we are dead while saying we are alive, lest we are dark while saying we are light. **5.** For thus the wise men said, 'There is indeed no wrath like this, that a man is sinful while yet his heart finds no fault with him that he may renounce his sins and his iniquities'. **6.** But whenever we keep the commandments of the Lord Jesus and hear his words,

23 Rom. 14. 20. 24 Cf. Prov. 20. 14. 25 Cf. Ps. 62. 11. 26 Ps. 118. 21. 27 Ps. 118. 118. 28 Ps. 118. 155. 29 Jer. 23. 24. 30 Cf. Ps. 110. 10, Prov. 1. 7. 31 Cf. Prov. 23. 12.

our way shall be straight and we shall not stumble. **7.** This too we were told by the psalmist, who says, 'Wherewith shall a young man straighten his way? By keeping your words'[32], he said. Woe to us indeed, if we forget the words of our fathers which they enjoined on us.

V. **1.** But with great pain and grief I ask like this, where is our freedom which exists in our monastery every day, and the liberty in which there is no deceit, deceit and theft being unknown
* p. 77 to us? **2.** So woe to those who steal * anything anywhere and who buy and sell with deceit and duplicity, not having first reported it. And those who do these and other things are cursed, because they were not ashamed and did not fear the curses which our father pronounced concerning such things. **3.** Therefore all the grief of our fathers and of all the saints and of our Lord Jesus shall come upon them and upon their pate. **4.** For we were taught and told that, 'The night is far spent, the day is at hand, let us therefore forsake the works of darkness and put upon us the armour of light'[33], which are good and righteous works, before that day of our end comes upon us suddenly like a snare[34] and we do not escape, **5.** for there will be no one who will hear us and no one who will wipe our tears from our eyes[35], because we did not hear diligently nor did we heed when they commanded us, saying, 'Cease from your wickednesses, learn to do good'[36]. 'But they have been disobedient', it is said, 'and have provoked his holy spirit to anger, and the Lord has turned to them in enmity'[37]. **6.** For thus said those of understanding when they saw that we were not examining ourselves or judging whether Christ Jesus was in us, 'Many', they said, 'are troubled in the communal life, for their lack of judgement has killed them'. **7.** But it is also said[38], 'If we heed the scriptures we shall know with certainty that to those who are disobedient time after time no right thing happens before God, but they endure months of vanity[39] in this world'. **8.** Again it is said[40], 'Behold, we have seen from the holy scriptures that those who follow the will of God shall inherit his good things, but those

32 Ps. 118. 9. 33 Rom. 13. 12. 34 Cf. Lk. 21. 34. 35 Cf. perhaps Rev. 7. 17. 36 Is. 1. 16-17. 37 Is. 63. 10. 38 For the following quotation, cf. p. 24. 39 Cf. Job 7. 3. 40 For the following quotation, cf. p. 8.

who walk in the evil will of their hearts are ripe * for wrath, as it is written, "Their worm shall not die and their fire shall not be quenched and they shall be for all flesh to see them" '[41]. * p. 78

VI. 1. So woe to us. Our disobedience will teach us, and our wickedness will upbraid us. Know and see that it is bitter for us to forsake the statutes of God[42] and the commandments of our fathers. 2. On no account then let it be said of us in wrath, 'Sow wheat and reap thorns'[43] — this great curse because of our ignorance and our disobedience, because we forsook the fountain of wisdom, and our ignorant hearts were darkened[44], so that we did not call to mind our end and the time when we shall give our spirit into the hands of God[45]. 3. Who then is wise and knows these things? and prudent and understands them? For the ways of the Lord are straight and the righteous shall walk in them; but the ungodly shall faint therein[46].

[Fragment 27] *TO THE BRETHREN ON MAINTAINING UNITY*

Besa, this most humble one, writes to his beloved brethren in the Lord.

I. 1. If I say 'Joyful Greetings', now where indeed is the joy? For the consolation was hidden from the eyes of those who desire our[1] salvation and who are grieved over our perdition, because some among us have become comparable to the ungodly man who has no joy and like the ignorant folk, because they have followed the devil who destroyed the world in his sins, as it was said, 'For some already followed after Satan'[2]. 2. And they have forsaken the law of God. They have followed their dark minds, which are in confusion, and their false knowledge, which is dark, and that which is wisdom in their own eyes, which those of understanding have demolished, 3. as it has been said, 'Woe unto them that are wise in their own eyes, and prudent in their own sight[3]. Woe * unto them who count darkness for light and light for darkness, who * p. 79

41 Is. 66. 24. 42 Cf. Jer. 2. 19. 43 Jer. 12. 13. 44 Cf. Rom. 1. 21. 45 Cf. Lk. 23. 46. 46 Hos. 14. 10.

1 Lit. : 'their'. I have here adopted the reading of the text parallel in Paris 130[5], 110, which makes better sense. 2 I Tim. 5. 15. 3 Is. 5. 21.

say that bitter is sweet and sweet is bitter'[4]. **4.** And again the apostle says, 'Their ignorant hearts were darkened. Saying, "We are wise", they became fools'[5], knowing neither what they said nor upon what they were established. **5.** And, making manifest also the shame and the disgrace of the people of this kind, and their self-sufficiency, it is said, 'As they did not think fit to have God in their knowledge, God gave them over to a reprobate mind to do those things which are unseemly, being filled with all iniquity, and wickedness, and evil, and covetousness, being full of envy, and murder, and strife, and deceit, and malignity; whisperers, slanderers, haters of God, despisers, proud, boasters, seekers after evil, who disobey their parents, senseless, unbelieving, cruel, merciless; who, knowing God's ordinance that those who do these things are worthy of death, not only do them but also approve of those who do them'[6]. **6.** And on this it has also been said, 'But the ways of the ungodly are dark, and they do not know how they stumble'[7], and, 'Death will befall the ignorant, and the ungodly will die in sins. Uncleannesses will defile a pestilent man on an evil and troublous day until he perishes'[8].

II. **1.** Truly according to the word of the apostle, 'I marvel that you so quickly turn from him who called you in the grace of Christ Jesus unto another gospel, whereas it is not another'[9]. **2.** So they too now turn away from good to evil, and from love and peace to hatred and enmity, and from humility and obedience to pride and disobedience, and from gentleness and enlightenment to hardness of heart and ignorance, and from truth and freedom to untruth and theft, and from purity to impurity, and from all the righteousness of God unto lawlessness and deceit and evil-speaking and whispering like a serpent, **3.** destroying the hearts of those who encounter them, deceiving those of like mind who resemble them in whispering and evil-speaking, maligning each
* p. 80 other, saying * what is not so or rather not revealing what is, and having spoken to many often with wrangling and vain deceit and hatred and mockery, gathering many sins up for themselves, and not even once saying what ought to be said in order that we may

[4] Is. 5. 20. [5] Rom. 1. 21-22. [6] Rom. 1. 28-32. [7] Prov. 4. 19. [8] Prov. 24. 8-10. [9] Gal. 1. 6-7.

be without sin. **4.** Therefore, brethren, let us depart from such things and [10] these deceitful counsels, that God may not be angry with us and cast us together with those who work lawlessness [11] and bring upon us suffering from this place on, even before we reach the place to which we shall go, the place of all suffering and groaning. **5.** Truly, according to the saying of our father, this is not our ideal, this is not our ideal [12], because we were not called unto defilement and strife but in purity [13] that we might live in propriety and in attendance upon the Lord honourably without anxiety [14].

III. **1.** Now therefore, brethren, all who like to display fellowship, be strong of heart, do not pay heed to these ignorant men who are among you, who cause stumbling, and who divide the body in pieces as it is written, 'A perverse man spreads strife and kindles the flame of deceit with evils and divides friends [15] and kinsmen', **2.** but rather pay heed to what the apostle has said, 'We command you in the name of our Lord Jesus Christ to withdraw yourselves from every brother who walks disorderly and not according to the teaching which they received from us' [16]. **3.** And again, 'We hear concerning some that they walk among you disorderly, they do no work but are busybodies' [17], speaking unseemly things, murmuring, and speaking evil in the corners of the monasteries, and in the streets, and in the houses, and on the roofs, and at their own places, with those of like mind in whispering, and in the talkativeness which has taken command of them. **4.** Concerning this it has been said, 'You shall not escape sin' [18]. They please not God and resist every man [19]. **5.** For these, indeed, are those about whom it has been said, * 'Evil men burn a city' [20], and again, 'These are the men who think of vanity and take evil counsel in this city' [21]. * p. 81

IV. **1.** But you who create these disturbances and forsake the

[10] ⲛⲉⲓ̈ϩⲃⲏⲩⲉ ⲛ̄ⲧⲉⲓ̈ϩⲉ ⲙⲛ̄ ('such things and') are written in smaller characters, badly faded, perhaps erased. They form the last line of a page, i.e. col. II, l. 30, of which col. I has 29 lines. The passage reads smoothly with or without this line. [11] Cf. Ps. 124. 5. [12] The repetition of this clause may be either due to dittography, or else for emphasis. [13] Cf. I Thes. 4. 7. [14] Cf. I Cor. 7. 35. [15] Prov. 16. 28. [16] II Thes. 3. 6. [17] II Thes. 3. 11. [18] Prov. 10. 19. [19] I Thes. 2. 15. [20] Prov. 29. 8. [21] Ez. 11. 2.

commandments of our fathers and their teachings, woe to you. What shall you do on the day of visitation? For your affliction is coming from afar, and to whom will you flee to help you?[22] **2.** Or will you raise evils and rebellions like the sons of this age in the holy monasteries of God? Shall we add sin upon sin? How did we know that God had forgiven us? **3.** For is not the time which is past sufficient, that is to say when we were in the world in the time of our bestiality, when we were walking in defilements and drunkennesses and revellings and carousals and abominable idolatries[23], walking in wickedness and envy, hateful and hating one another[24], disobedient, erring[25], walking in the vanity of our hearts, darkened in our thoughts, alienated from the life of God because of the ignorance which was in us and because of our obstinacy, having given ourselves up to defilement and the performance of every uncleanness in covetousness? **4.** Now we were not taught in this manner[26], but rather thus were we taught : — 'Work out your salvation in fear and trembling. For it is God who works in you the will and the fulfilment of the will'[27]. **5.** And, 'Do all things without murmuring and disputing, that you may become sinless and innocent, children of God, holy, in the midst of the crooked and perverse generation among whom you are manifested even as the enlighteners in the world'[28]. **6.** And, 'You were called unto freedom, brethren, only let not our freedom become an occasion of the flesh, but through the love of the Spirit serve one another'[29]. **7.** And again when we were taught we were bidden, 'Now therefore renounce all these, anger, wrath, wickedness; let not a shameful word come out of your mouth. Do not lie one to another, having stripped off the old man with his works, and having put on the new'[30].

* p. 82 V. **1.** But now we have turned judgement into gall and * the fruit of righteousness into bitterness[31], despising our fathers and lying to each other in hatred, conflict, and strife for the sake of carnal foods, although we have not been short of anything we needed. **2.** And even if we have been short, we remember the word

[22] Cf. Is. 10. 3. [23] Cf. I Pet. 4. 3. [24] Tit. 3. 3. [25] Cf. Tit. 3. 3. [26] Cf. Eph. 4. 17-20. [27] Phil. 2. 12-13. [28] Phil. 2. 14-15. [29] Gal. 5. 13. [30] Col. 3. 8-10. [31] Cf. Amos 6. 12.

which is written, 'In straits for Christ's sake'[32]. And we despise the grace of God who made us worthy to be brought into this life though we were not worthy of it, so that we became an offence to the Jews and to the Greeks and to the church of God[33], bringing shame on those that have (it) not, and so that those who are near us and those who are far from us hear and say, 'Behold, they too hate each other, our way is their way', as it is written, 'Because of you my name is blasphemed among the Gentiles'[34]. **3.** Thus again the beloved of God, Apa Athanasius, said[35], 'Do not let anyone see you behaving unseemly and say, "This is the man who disciplines himself to attain the gift that belongs unto heaven. This is the disciple and the pupil of the wise teacher. This is the man who was chosen out of the world, having been reckoned with the angels of heaven, he who expects the king of heaven, hoping to stand by his side!" ' **4.** And, 'Let Christ be glorified by you; do not let him be blasphemed because of you. For it is said, "I will honour him who honours me, but I will despise him who will despise me" '[36]. **5.** And he proclaimed the word which decides openly, 'You also despise him even if you honour him with your words but blaspheme him by your works'.

VI. **1.** Now, brethren, on no account let God be blasphemed because of us, and the name of our fathers be defamed[37] because of our ignorance in forsaking their teachings and their commandments which they enjoined upon us, and their wisdom and their purity, in that * they bade us, adjuring us by heaven and earth, * p. 83
that we should not transgress them from the least to the greatest, and especially that we should not destroy our body in any evil way, lest we repent at our end and break our hearts in the place to which we shall go. **2.** We know that it is at all times necessary for

[32] Cf. II Cor. 12. 10. [33] Cf. I Cor. 10. 32. [34] Is. 52. 5, cf. Rom. 2. 24.
[35] The following quotations do not occur in the published works of Athanasius but form part of a Sah. homily the author of which is unidentified, cf. Ryl. 62, 2v, ll. 18-27, cf. also BM 990, 4v. For arguments in favour of attributing the homily to Athanasius, cf. L. TH. LEFORT, 'Un nouveau "De virginitate" attribué à S. Athanase', *Analecta Bollandiana*, LXVII, pp. 142 ff. The texts are edited by L. TH. LEFORT, *S. Athanase, Lettres Festales et Pastorales*, CSCO, 150/Copt.19, Louvain, 1955, pp. 121 ff., cf. also pp. XXXI ff. [36] I Kg. 2. 30.
[37] Lit. : 'destroyed' hence 'defamed', but perhaps emend to read : 'despised', cf. p. 23.

us all to stand at the judgement-seat of Christ and for each one to receive through his body according to the things he has done whether good or evil [38]. **3.** 'But let our eyes look at things that are upright', as it is written, 'and our eyelids open wide to the truths' [39]. And let us incline our hearts to teaching and prepare our ears for the words of knowledge [40], and write them on the tables of our hearts [41], that we may escape like a gazelle out of a snare and like a bird out of a trap [42], and that we may escape from filth and uncleanness. **4.** We remember that which was said, 'From now the axe is laid at the root of the trees; every tree then which does not bear good fruit shall be cut down and cast into the fire' [43]. **5.** For on this it has been said, 'The end of all is nigh. Be prudent therefore and be sober unto prayers' [44]. And again, 'Be sober and vigilant because your adversary the devil goes, roaring as the lions, seeking to devour your souls' [45]. And we did not trouble about it, nor did our heart know how to perceive what was fitting. **6.** Let us therefore stand in awe, and remember that it has been said, 'Give glory to the Lord your God before the darkness comes and your feet stumble upon the dark mountains. You will look for light, a shadow of death is there, and they shall be put in darkness. But if you do not hear, your soul will weep secretly, confronted with your shame, and your eyes will shed tears' [46].

VII. **1.** Therefore, brethren, depart from provoking the wrath of God. This means not corrupting the mind of anyone against
* p. 84 him who teaches him, nor despising your fathers, lest the * Lord Christ be angry with you and bring a curse upon you from this place on, because it is written, 'He who ill-treats his father and his mother, thinking, "I do not sin", is an associate of an ungodly man' [47]. **2.** And, 'He who shall revile his father and his mother, let him die the death' [48]. And, 'Cursed is he who shall despise his father' [49], who takes care of him, or his fathers, who teach him, in pride, mockery, hatred, and boastfulness. **3.** They [50] do not remember how they [51] received us in their love for God's sake, so

[38] Cf. II Cor. 5. 10. [39] Cf. Prov. 4. 25. [40] Cf. Prov. 23. 12. [41] Cf. Prov. 7. 3. [42] Cf. Prov. 6. 5. [43] Lk. 3. 9, cf. Mt. 3. 10. [44] I Pet. 4. 7. [45] I Pet. 5. 8. [46] Jer. 13. 16-17. [47] Prov. 28. 24. [48] Cf. Ex. 21. 16, Lev 20. 9, Mt. 15. 4, Mk. 7. 10. [49] Deut. 27. 16. [50] I.e. those who despise their fathers. [51] I.e. the fathers.

that we might benefit our souls. And did we not give a reminder and did they not call to mind that it had been said, 'He who shall recompense evil for good, evil will not stir from his house'? [52] **4.** Therefore let us pay heed not to corrupt the mind of anyone, nor to despise your fathers, because such things are great sins. **5.** For our fathers also said that it was written in a certain place, 'Wash your heart from wickedness, Jerusalem, that you may be saved' [53]. 'And you shall find those men', they said, 'washing away righteousness and sowing in themselves wickedness and disobedience' [54].

VIII. **1.** Have you not heard, O man, the saying, 'Woe to him who gives his neighbour to drink with evil corruption from such things as he conceives not, and makes him drunk' [55] with evil-speaking, disobedience, and disaffection? **2.** We weakly act as a drag on one another instead of being an edification to each other, 'edifying one another' [56] and 'speaking to one another in psalms and hymns and spiritual songs' [57], as it is written. **3.** But we have become mutually destructive with the devil's works because the fear of God is far from those who do these things. **4.** Truly if they and others like them were only children the grief would be small, but since they are grown men who act thus, therefore it is a great sorrow. **5.** For they have resembled those who murmured against * Moses at that time, being notable men, but not revering him even (* p. 85) after he had taken great troubles with them and brought them out of the house of their bondage, so that the earth opened its mouth and swallowed them up [58]. **6.** They did not remember how he prayed for them before God, saying, 'If you will forgive their sin, forgive it, but if not, blot me out of your book which you have written' [59]; nor did they remember how he commanded them by his word, 'Give heed to the matter of leprosy' [60] which means evil-speaking. **7.** You do not know that our stability is through each other, and so also is our destruction through each other.

IX. **1.** Hear that it has been said, 'If you have understanding, answer your neighbour; if not, lay your hand upon your mouth' [61],

52 Prov. 17. 13. 53 Jer. 4. 14. 54 Cf. p. 44. 55 Cf. Hab. 2. 15.
56 I Thes. 5. 11. 57 Eph. 5. 19. 58 Cf. Num. 16. 2 ff. 59 Ex. 32. 32.
60 Deut. 24. 8. 61 Ecclus. 5. 12.

and, 'To speak a word in its season is altogether good'[62]. **2.** Moreover, if there is anyone whose heart is grieved in anything, who prevents him from sensibly and wisely telling it to your fathers? And there will be no sorrow, but rather they will rejoice the more at the frankness conferred by the state of being a son and a brother. **3.** For by means of these things unanimity is revealed, because there is no division in our hearts, one to another, but we vigilantly keep our tongue from all evil-speaking[63], since he who guards his mouth and his tongue, guards his soul[64], and he who loves life will restrain his mouth[65]. **4.** Also, 'Death and life are in the power of the tongue and he who controls it shall be satisfied with its fruits'[66]. Again, 'Groan not at one another, my brethren'[67]. You know that we shall all receive a great judgement. Behold, the judge stands at the door[68], that he may judge each one according to his works[69]. **5.** Are these things unimportant, to which the wicked and deceitful men have set their hand, even going so far in their bond of deceit as to compose notices for publication which stir up rebellions and cause division of the brethren? For they fear not * p. 86 God, as it is written, * 'Bloody and deceitful men shall not remember their days'[70]. **6.** Is there not amongst you a man or a woman, a boy or a girl, like an angel? And is it not angelic to guard one's heart and body from all foulness and impurity and one's tongue from falsehood and chatter and for one's constancy to be true? **7.** And there is a man or woman or boy or girl like a devil. And is it not devilish to defile one's heart and one's body with all uncleanness, and one's tongue with evil-speaking and deceit and one's constancy with lying? **8.** Is it not those things, deceitful, hateful, and discordant, which deliver you up to him who ensnares you to your doom, O unclean and pestilent men, as it is written, 'The deceitful shall be for a prey'?[71] **9.** Again, you are ensnared by one another, and you make a pit for one another until Satan looks gloatingly[72] at you and tramples upon you by means of

[62] Cf. perhaps Prov. 15. 23 (especially the Hebrew text). [63] Cf. Wisd. 1. 11. [64] Prov. 21. 23. [65] Prov. 16. 17. [66] Cf. Prov. 18. 21. [67] Jam. 5. 9. [68] Jam. 5. 9. [69] Cf. I Pet. 1. 17. [70] Ps. 54. 24. — Cf. p. 21, n. 2. [71] Prov. 12. 24. [72] Lit. : 'fill eye', hence 'look intently', cf. CRUM, *Dictionary*, p. 73 b, perhaps better 'gaze one's fill'. It often seems to indicate not the intensity of the look so much as the fact that it is accompanied by

these abominable works, and so you are entangled in his nets [73].

X. **1.** Do not think that I hate you,, when I say these things : truly I love you greatly. I counsel you as a brother that you may repent and escape the snares of the devil, as it is written, 'You will bring me out of this snare which they have hidden for me, for you are my protector' [74], **2.** and again, 'The righteous escapes out of nets' [75]; and that we may be worthy to speak the word which is written, 'Do not rejoice over me, my enmity, because I fell; I shall rise again' [76]. **3.** Now therefore, brethren, all of you together keep yourselves in the love of God [77], in order that you may not be led in the error of the lawless and fall from your steadfastness [78], that is to say your constancy which is full of all wisdom. And be vigilant, stand fast in the faith, be strong and mighty, let all your works be in love [79]. **4.** And again as the apostle has said, 'I beseech you my brethren that you mark those who make divisions and scandals contrary to the teaching which you have learned, and withdraw yourselves from them. For such are not the servants of the Lord Christ, but * of their belly. And through * p. 87
their fair speech and flattery they beguile the hearts of the innocent' [80]. **5.** And again, 'Beware of the dogs, beware of the evil workers' [81], beware of the men over whom the demons have ruled. Do not let them give you occasion for stumbling. **6.** For on this the apostle said, 'I speak by way of reproach [82]. For you, being wise, bear willingly with the foolish. For you bear with him who beguiles you, him who turns away, him who enslaves you, devours, and seizes, him who exalts himself, him who smites you in the face' [83]. **7.** Is it not a great sin that you buy and sell with the laymen, contrary to the judgement of your fathers who take care of you? It is especially laid down by our fathers from the beginning that men shall not buy or sell contrary to their judgement. **8.** And again our fathers, who have now gone to God, ordered

an emotion, usually joy, and often malicious. 73 For a passage of striking similarity to the above (beginning : 'Is there not amongst you a man') cf. MS. Copte, No. 2, ⲥϥ-ⲥ̄ⲓϥⲁ (Institut français d'archéologie orientale, Cairo), an unedited Shenoute MS. Unfortunately I have had the opportunity to study only parts of this most interesting MS. 74 Ps. 30. 5. 75 Prov. 11. 8. 76 Mic. 7. 8. 77 Jude 21. 78 II Pet. 3. 17. 79 I Cor. 16. 13-14. 80 Rom. 16. 17-18. 81 Phil. 3. 2. 82 II Cor. 11. 21. 83 II Cor. 11. 19-20.

and commanded saying, 'Cursed is he who shall buy and sell covertly without his fathers'.

XI. **1.** But you, elders, take care of the men under you who are entrusted to you and who are your children, since you received them for the sake of God. **2.** Take care also of their souls in the love of God, because it is written, 'I exhort therefore the elders who are among you, as fellow-elder and as witness of the sufferings of Christ, and as steward [84] of the glory which shall be revealed. Tend the flock of God which is among you, not under constraint but willingly according to God; not with love of shameful gain but gladly; not as being lord over the charges but being examples to the flock' [85]. **3.** You remember that it was said, 'Freely I will be spent for your souls' [86], and, 'To whom much is entrusted, from him will much be required' [87], that you may care for their souls according to God and not leave them lacking that which is needful for our way of life; **4.** because it has been said, 'If there is a brother or a sister naked and lacking daily food, and one among you say to them, "Go in peace and be warmed and be satisfied", but does not give them the things of the body which they need, what is the
* p. 88 use?' [88] **5.** If, however, they do not lack food and clothing, * they have no complaint to make [89], and you yourself also will be sinless. **6.** But be vigilant not to let them prefer one more than another, lest you find some being at their ease because they have a friend, but others walking in distress and grief because they have no friend. Therefore it is a great sin in such a place that they should favour some and neglect others, not regarding them at all. **7.** But let there be the same equality [90] for all of them together as it is written, 'He who had much did not exceed, and he who had little did not lack' [91], in order that there may be peace for them all and in order that they may serve God in contentment, without faultfinding or favouritism.

XII. **1.** And you, fathers of the houses, in the fear of God take care of the men whom God entrusted to you, teaching them for the salvation of their souls. For it has been said, 'Fathers, do not

[84] Probably in error for 'partaker', the N.T. reading. [85] I Pet. 5. 1-3. [86] Cf. II Cor. 12. 15. [87] Lk. 12. 48. [88] Jam. 2. 15-16. [89] Lit. : 'no word to say'. [90] Cf. II Cor. 8. 14. [91] II Cor. 8. 15, cited from Ex. 16. 18.

provoke your children to wrath but nurture them in the teaching and the instruction of the Lord'[92], **2.** and again, 'He to whom a man is entrusted, of him he shall be required. Likewise he to whom no man is entrusted, his own soul shall be required of him'[93] **3.** You know that even as he who received five talents worked with them and gained another five, and as he who received two gained another two[94], so also are you if you tend them well like the good shepherd who lays down his life for his sheep[95]. **4.** For the Lord says, 'There is no love greater than this that a man lay down his life for his friends'[96], in order that you and they together may be worthy to go into the bridechamber with the true bridegroom[97], Jesus. **5.** Take heed and be vigilant, do not let one of us be found whose garment is filthy or perished and it be said to him with shame, 'Friend, how did you come hither, without wearing a wedding-garment?'[98] or it be said, 'Cast him out into the outer darkness'[99]. Woe to me and woe to everyone if this befall us!

XIII. **1.** But you, O brethren, obey your fathers who teach you with all proper obedience and submission, because it has been said, 'Submit to one another in the fear * of Christ'[100], and, 'Children, * p. 89 obey your fathers in every respect, for this is the will of the Lord'[101], **2.** and again, 'Obey your great ones and submit to them, for they themselves keep vigil for your souls, that they may do so with joy and not groan'[102], **3.** and again, 'But we beseech you, brethren, to know those that labour among you and preside over you in the Lord and teach you, and to esteem them highly in love because of their work'[103], that you may become a crown of pride and a joy of glory to those who see us and all those who shall meet us, for a conversion and a repentance, and that you may become the pride of all our fathers on the day of Christ, that is, when we come out of this world and find freedom in their presence in that place. **4.** Therefore, brethren, let us turn and establish our works and our ways, and seek the eternal ways of the Lord, that we may find purification for our souls[104]. **5.** And the Lord Christ Jesus, the Son of the Blessed, God of hosts, the Almighty, shall direct your

92 Eph. 6. 4. 93 I cannot identify this quotation. 94 Cf. Mt. 25. 16-17. 95 Cf. Jn. 10. 11. 96 Cf. Jn. 15. 13. 97 Cf. Mt. 25. 10. 98 Mt. 22. 12. 99 Cf. Mt. 22. 13. 100 Eph. 5. 21. 101 Col. 3. 20. 102 Cf. Heb. 13. 17. 103 I Thes. 5. 12-13. 104 Cf. Jer. 6. 16.

hearts towards the love of God and the patience of Christ [105]. **6.** And he will give all of you together power, whether great or small, father or son, mother or daughter, or everyone together, to support each other in order that you may fulfil the laws of Christ [106]. **7.** And the God of peace will crush Satan quickly under your feet [107], and he will give all of you power to perform his will, doing that which is pleasing amongst us before him through Jesus Christ; and he will fill you with every good desire [108] that you may become wise in respect of good, but innocent in respect of evil [109].

XIV. **1.** Furthermore, I shall also tell you this saying, which is no loss to you but rather a profit and a glory, and that is this: that in the forty days during which it is proclaimed in all the earth that everyone in the whole world should strive with himself, each one according to his strength, be he great or small, and even going beyond his strength, **2.** I hear that many among you in whom
* p. 90 there is strength to excel eat every evening, * and care not that these days are one thing and all the other days another, while many laymen outside do periods of two days together or four, and also that some fast a week; **3.** especially the brethren of this monastery with us, not only do they all act as a team from the old men who have no strength down to the little children who are small, but also most of them fast four days or a week without even eating bread, **4.** remembering that our Lord Jesus [110], and Moses [111] too, and Elijah [112], did the whole forty days on end without tasting anything, either bread or water. **5.** But we have not resembled them in the very least. What is the use [113] of our having retired from the world into this life of which we are not worthy? **6.** So let us not be negligent, but let us all strive, each one according to his strength, even as the Lord said, 'Strive to go in through the narrow gate' [114], of which he said, 'Few are they who will go in by it [115]. But many are they who go through the wide gate' [116]. **7.** This means: those who do their hearts' desire now, as they wish, are many; but they will break their hearts when they leave this world. On the other

105 II Thes. 3. 5. 106 Cf. Gal. 6. 2. 107 Rom. 16. 20. 108 II Thes. 1. 11. 109 Rom. 16. 19. 110 Cf. Mt. 4. 2, Lk. 4. 2. 111 Cf. Ex. 34. 28. 112 Cf. III Kg. 19. 8. 113 Lit.: 'greater part', 'greatness', but here as if ϩⲏⲩ 'profit', 'usefulness'; for examples of this use of ϩⲟⲩⲟ, cf. CRUM, *Dictionary*, p. 735 a. 114 Lk. 13. 24. 115 Cf. Mt. 7. 14. 116 Cf. Mt. 7. 13.

hand, they who will be distressed and grieved for God's sake are few; but they will receive their comfort and their hearts' content in the place to which they will go.

XV. **1.** Again the Lord says, 'He who finds his life will lose it, but he who loses his life for my sake will find it unto eternal life'[117]. **2.** May it come to pass that the Lord grant that we be found vigilant[118] and fruitful, remembering his commandments, purging ourselves of every impurity, hesitancy[119], youthful quarrelsomeness, and arrogance which God resists[120]. **3.** We are quite satisfied with the sound teaching of our fathers and their commandments which they have enjoined on us in order that you may become worthy to enter the life together, you, your sons, your brethren, your mothers, your daughters, and all your kin, there being nothing to cause you to stumble. **4.** For indeed, I have not written these things * to teach you. For I myself am a wretched man, not having attained to these measures, and I pray[121] for myself that God may deliver me from every evil, for I am a poor man and a miserable. But I desire us all to escape the judgement of God and become worthy of eternal life together. * p. 91

[Fragment 28] *TO MATTHEW*

Besa the most humble writes to his beloved brother Matthew.

I. **1.** I marvel that you have turned so quickly from the grace of Jesus Christ[1], who called you out of the darkness into the light[2] and from death into life, having forsaken your constancy and your monastic way of life. **2.** You have disowned your very self through weakness and disaffection. You loved this present age and went to Thessalonica[3], which is foolishness and the way in which you turned shamefully back so as to become a stumbling-block for many. **3.** You did not remember the word of the Lord, how he said, 'He who will offend one of these little ones who believe in me, it is better for him that a millstone should be tied to his neck and he be

117 Mt. 10. 39 and Jn. 12. 25. 118 Cf. Lk. 12. 37. 119 Lit. : 'double-mindedness'. 120 Cf. Prov. 3. 34, I Pet. 5. 5, Jam. 4. 6. 121 Lit. : 'you pray' (fem. sg.). The emendation seems necessary as the letter is addressed to monks.

1 Cf. Gal. 1. 6. 2 Cf. I Pet. 2. 9. 3 Cf. II Tim. 4. 10.

sunk in the depth of the sea[4], rather than that he should offend one of these little ones who believe in me'[5]. **4.** For truly, it is not a small offence which has befallen many through you, for they were amazed at what you did, in that you have acted wickedly against yourself. You have forsaken the fountain of living water and have dug for yourself broken cisterns which will not be able to hold water[6]. **5.** You did not consider nor did you learn to understand that the thing that you have undertaken to do was a disgrace to you in the sight of everyone. **6.** Nor again did you remember what the Lord said, 'He who will endure to the end, he shall be saved'[7], and, 'In your constancy you shall win your souls'[8]. Thus again, 'The crown is for those who shall endure'[9].

II. **1.** Can it be that these things are profitable to you? It is you who know. The Lord shall return to everyone his righteousness and his faithfulness[10]. **2.** * If the fact was that your heart was grieved about something or that I pained you unwittingly contrary to the commandment of God, why did you not tell me that I might know? **3.** For neither I, nor you, nor anyone else, knows any evil that I did you. For I have done no injury nor have I corrupted anybody, nor have I robbed anybody. The Lord is witness and also all the brethren know of every deed and every word. **4.** If I am an evil-doer preventing men from doing the will of God, can you say it of your sons?[11] Who pursued them except on their own account, because of their evil works? But each one is responsible. As for me, I am innocent of the blood of everyone[12]. For it is written, 'I will honour him who will honour me, but I will despise him who will despise me'[13]. **5.** But also concerning your sons you ought to remember the word which the Lord has spoken, 'He who loves son and daughter more than me is not worthy of me. And he who will not take up his cross and follow me is not worthy of me'[14]. **6.** And again, 'What will man profit if he gain the whole world but forfeit his soul? Or what shall man give in exchange for his soul?'[15] **7.** Do not think then, O brother, that it is an honour for

* p. 92

4 Mt. 18. 6. 5 Cf. Lk. 17. 2. 6 Cf. Jer. 2. 13. 7 Mt. 10. 22, Mt. 24. 13, Mk. 13. 13. 8 Lk. 21. 19. 9 Zech. 6. 14. 10 I Kg. 26. 23. 11 This probably means : 'can you say that your sons are so prevented by me?' 12 Acts 20. 26. 13 I Kg. 2. 30. 14 Mt. 10. 37-38. 15 Mt. 16. 26, Mk. 8. 36.

you that you have denied your constancy or that you have forsaken the community of your fathers who nurtured you therein. **8.** You did not remember my reverend father, nor did you remember your sons, nor yet did you remember the men for whom you prayed until you brought them in. But even after having run away secretly like a thief do you suppose, then, that you can thus derive profit?

III. **1.** The apostle says, in commending those who shall vigorously perfect their constancy, 'Let us hold fast the confession of hope undeviating, for he is faithful who promised. And let us look to one another for an encouragement to love and good works, not forsaking our assembly as the custom of some is, but exhorting, and all the more so, as you see the day approaching. For if we sin wilfully after receiving knowledge of the truth, there will no more remain sacrifice for sin. But it is a fearful thing to expect the judgement and the fierceness[16] of the fire which will devour the adversaries'[17]. **2.** And again, 'It is a fearful thing to fall into the hands of the living God'[18]. **3.** * And he also said, 'Remember the former days in which you were enlightened, having endured a great conflict of sufferings. So you are on the one hand mocked with reproaches and tribulations, and on the other hand also you have become partakers with those who are thus (used). For you even suffered with those who are bound, and the spoiling of your possessions you accepted joyfully, knowing that you have a better possession which abides. Therefore cast not your boldness away, which has great recompense of reward. For you have need of constancy, in order that, having done the will of God, you may receive the promise'[19]. **4.** You see therefore, friend and brother, that he who will do the will of God and perfect his constancy, shall receive the promise. **5.** Therefore I say to you, do not persuade yourself thus : you shall not profit, for there is no profit in what you do. I am anxious for you thus, lest you be past repentance at your end.

* p. 93

IV. **1.** Moreover the Lord says of those who turn back in disaffection, 'I planted you as a vine wholly bearing true fruit. How did you turn to bitterness, vine that became strange?'[20] **2.** And again, 'What is the way of Egypt to you that you drink of the

[16] Cf. p. 8, n. 35. [17] Heb. 10. 23-27. [18] Heb. 10. 31. [19] Heb. 10. 32-36.
[20] Jer. 2. 21.

water of Geon[21] which is turbid[22]; and what is the way of Assyria to you that you drink water from their rivers? Your disobedience will teach you and your wickedness will upbraid you. Know and see that it is bitter for you to forsake me[23]. **3.** For of old you broke your yoke and burst your bonds. You said, "I will not be a servant" '[24]. Do not think that I hate you, saying these things, but know rather that I wish you to return to your monastery in peace, that you may not forfeit your soul in your old age. **4.** For who amongst all those who have left us did not regret it, that you should not regret it? Or who benefited, that you should benefit? The act of desertion which you have committed, does it not disclose whom you contend with or with whom you take counsel? **5.** Rightly
* p. 94 then it was said, 'Let everyone beware * of his neighbour, and do not trust your brethren, because every brother will utterly supplant[25] and every friend will walk craftily. Everyone will mock his friend and they will not speak the truth, because their tongue was taught to speak lies'[26]. **6.** Did we send you on a mission in order that you might go and lose your soul? For we, in fact, chose you as an earnest man, and sent you. If your mind was not at rest about your going, why did you not tell us that we might know and not send you?

V. **1.** Nevertheless, know that it has been said, 'Hearken therefore now and hear; they were not speaking thus openly, for no man is repenting of his wickedness saying, "What have I done?" The runner has ceased from his course like a horse with his sweat on him from his neighing'[27]. Do not, therefore, let it be said, 'The way of the daughter of my people is not towards uprightness nor

21 I.e. the Nile, cf. J. HASTINGS, *A Dictionary of the Bible*, Edinburgh, 1900 ff., II, p. 174, and IV, pp. 498 f. The LXX reads Γηών for the Hebrew שִׁחוֹר.
22 The clause 'which is turbid' has no equivalent in the Hebrew or the LXX. It appears to be a gloss on שִׁחוֹר (probably 'black' hence 'turbid'). 23 Jer. 2. 18-19. 24 Jer. 2. 20. 25 Lit. : 'will, with a tripping, trip up by the heels'. The construction can only be explained by reference to the Hebrew עָקוֹב יַעְקֹב, which is followed by the LXX *πτέρνῃ πτερνιεῖ*. As the Infinitive Absolute in Hebrew serves to strengthen the verb, I have translated 'utterly'. The Hebrew of Jer. 9. 4 would clearly call to mind the story of Jacob's naming (Gen. 25. 26) which is referred to elsewhere in the O.T. (e.g. Gen. 27. 36, Hos. 12. 3), but the pun has been lost in Greek and Coptic alike. 26 Jer. 9. 4-5. 27 Jer. 8. 6.

towards purity'[28]. **2.** And do not let it be said, 'Woe unto them who call evil good and good evil, who count darkness for light and light for darkness, who say that bitter is sweet and sweet is bitter. Woe unto them that are wise in their own eyes and prudent in their own sight'[29]. **3.** Do not therefore, my brother, lead yourself astray. Arise and search yourself like the woman whose coin[30] got lost; she swept her house, searching and looking around until she found it, and called her friends and neighbours saying, 'Rejoice with me because I have found my penny[31] which I lost'[32]. **4.** For many of the brethren amongst us did not waver in their constancy towards God when their sons and their brothers departed from us, since they knew that they would not find a son beside them, or a daughter, or any of those related to them by the flesh, in the time of their need, when they come into the hands of Christ. **5.** But it is the good that each one will have done that he will find beside him at that time. For father will not die for son, nor son for father, nor brother for brother, but everyone shall die for his own sin, and it is the teeth of him that eats sour grapes that shall be set on edge[33], as the scripture says. **6.** For if everyone thinks thus, weakly to become estranged as you * did, who will live with his fellows? (* p. 95) Unless our fathers had persevered in their constancy, where were we to find them that we might dwell with them? **7.** But now our fathers perfected their constancy and went to God. If we ourselves are like them, many will profit through us, but if we turn back and renounce our constancy, many will be lost because of us and stumble. **8.** Therefore, we exhort you through God and our Lord Jesus that you return to your monastery in order that your mind may be at rest and that you may profit and not obey those who advise you to forsake your monastery. For they will not be able to speak for you at the time of your need.

28 Jer. 4. 11. 29 Is. 5. 20-21. 30 Lit. : 'stater' which equals four drachmas. But when the coin is found it is called ϭⲓⲥⲕⲓⲧⲉ which is one drachma. It may therefore be assumed that the writer was not aware of the actual value of the coins and uses ⲥⲁⲧⲉⲉⲣⲉ to mean 'coin' or 'drachma'; cf. A. Böhlig, 'Die griechischen Lehnwörter im sahidischen und bohairischen Neuen Testament', *Studien zur Erforschung des christlichen Ägyptens*, Heft 2, p. 381. 31 Lit. : 'drachma'. 32 Cf. Lk. 15. 8-9. 33 Jer. 38. 30.

[Fragment 29] *TO ANTINOE*

Besa writes to Antinoe.

I. **1.** Although I have sent to you more than once to put this foolishness from you and restrain your boastful tongue and your lips, that they do not speak of things which are not so or which you do not know, yet, behold, you have not ceased nor left off up till now, but even added more in your scorn. **2.** He who despises his neighbour despises himself, and he who condemns his brother or his neighbour condemns himself and sins against his own soul. **3.** Those who fear the Lord restrain their mouth and do not reproach their brethren or their neighbours, but rather honour them the more and give them glory, knowing that he who guards his mouth and his tongue, guards his soul[1]. **4.** So therefore, I advise you as a brother to cease from this petulance by which you will not profit, and this pointless contempt in which there is no advantage, lest you regret on the day when every mouth will be shut and we shall all be under the judgement of God. **5.** For it was said, 'There are those who speak like piercing swords, but the tongues of the wise heal'[2]. Why do you despise your sister and reproach her? Will your heart be at ease if she departs because of you or at your instigation? Will you not grieve or be pained? Will you choose to bring down upon your head the word which
* p. 96 is written, * 'scarer of men'?[3] **6.** If you insult her, you insult yourself, and if you justify her, you justify yourself. If you understand the commandments of the Lord Jesus and heed them, you will understand what is seemly. Good counsel shall guard you and holy thought keep you, for it shall deliver you from every evil thing[4].

II. **1.** Nevertheless I tell you, if you do not abandon this foolish attitude and get you understanding, I will cause your heart to be grieved and I will no more forbear with you. **2.** The Lord said, 'If you love each other, everyone shall know that you are my disciples[5]. For he who hates his brother walks in darkness, not knowing where he is going because the darkness has closed his eyes'[6]. **3.** And it was also said, 'A wise woman builds a house,

[1] Prov. 21. 23. [2] Prov. 12. 18. [3] Cf. I Tim. 1. 10. — The Greek N.T. has: ἀνδραποδιστής. [4] Cf. Prov. 2. 11-12. [5] Cf. Jn. 13. 35. [6] Cf. I Jn. 2. 11.

but the foolish will destroy it with her hands'[7], which means that the wise woman encourages[8] her neighbour in the fear of God and the love which is in her heart towards her sister and her sisters. **4.** But, on the other hand, the foolish woman will destroy them by her words full of bitterness, hatred, wickedness, and scorn, even as it is written, 'A rod of scorn is in the mouth of the foolish'[9], and that means you. **5.** For he who loves life will restrain his mouth[10], but he who goads with words shall not be saved[11] Why do you think thus? Do you not hope to come into the hands of God? How long are you continuing to be so very foolish? **6.** You do not fear God, nor do you respect man[12], nor do you consider the forfeiting of your soul. 'The foolish pours out all his wrath'[13] and, 'The mouth of the foolish is ruin to him, and his lips are a snare to his soul'[14]. **7.** Do you not know that he who despises man to the extent of condemning him, despises God and scorns him? For man was made in the image of God[15] and such things are of the devilish enemy who envies us, hardening our hearts towards * one another with pride by which we shall not profit, since it has * p. 97 been said, 'Pride is an abomination in the sight of God[16], and as for the presumptuous and the boastful, Pestilence is his name'[17].

III. **1.** On this matter the man of God, Apa Antonius, said[18], 'While we are alone, they[19] make us sit in judgement on one another, even in their absence from us. With their slanders which they arrogantly plant[20] in our hearts, we are hard of heart and we decry one another, we are boastful to each other with our hard words, we are always troubled at heart, we blame one another and not ourselves, we think that our trouble comes through our[21] neighbours, we are judges of appearances while the arch-robber is inside the house; with quarrels and factions we fight each

7 Prov. 14. 1. 8 Lit. : 'builds'. 9 Prov. 14. 3. 10 Prov. 16. 17. 11 Prov. 19. 4. 12 Cf. Lk. 18. 2. 13 Prov. 29. 11. 14 Prov. 18. 7. 15 Cf. Gen. 1. 26-27. 16 Cf. Lk. 16. 15. 17 Prov. 21. 24. 18 For the following quotation, cf. J.-P. Migne, *Patrologiae Cursus Completus, Series Graeca*, Paris, 1857 ff., 40, 983 B f., also 40, 1012 B f. It also forms part of a longer quotation from Antony on p. 97. For the relationship between the various versions, cf. G. Garitte, 'A propos des lettres de S. Antoine l'Ermite', *Le Muséon*, LII, pp. 11 ff. 19 I.e. demons. 20 The quotation on p. 97 has : 'put'. 21 The quotation on p. 97 has wrongly : 'your'.

other[22], until we carry our point'. **2.** Therefore I declare to you before God that if you will not turn away from this contemptuousness, you too will be filled with grief. For I am so anxious for you that I do not wish that we may hear of your wickedness, or that your name may be evilly spoken of, or that harm may befall you. **3.** Now therefore, pay heed to teaching and prepare your ears for the words of knowledge[23], that you may have confidence in God[24]. And let your eyes look at things that are upright and your eyelids open wide to the truths[25], in order that you may learn what is fitting, and that you may understand that he who refrains from uttering a hard word is wise, and the patient man is wise[26]. **4.** So put this provocation to anger from you, and this petulance, and this contemptuousness, for it was said, 'The lips of the fool shall bring him into evils and his stubborn mouth invokes death'[27]. **5.** Therefore do not be foolish, but know what the will of the * p. 98 Lord is[28], and see which is the good way, * and walk in it, that you may find purification for your soul[29].

IV. **1.** For it has been said, 'The tongue is a little member and speaks great words'[30], and, 'A little fire sets much wood alight. The tongue also is a fire[31] which defiles the whole body and sets on fire the cycle of generation[32], and which is restless, evil, and full of deadly poison. With it we bless God the Father, and with it we curse men who were made in God's likeness'[33]. **2.** We have been told, 'These things ought not to be so'[34], and, 'Does a fountain send forth fresh and salty water from the same well?'[35] And, 'Can a fig tree bring forth olives or a vine bring forth figs, or shall salt be able to produce sweet water?'[36] **3.** It is meant by this that no creatures which God created change the likeness wherein he created them. But man, time and again, turns from the good to the evil, acting contrary to the command of God which he laid upon him, and he changes his nature contrary to the manner which the Lord God ordained for him. **4.** All creation is subject to God, whether mountains and hills, or the sea and the rivers,

22 Lit. : 'we fight each other in them'. It seems preferable to follow the reading on p. 98 and omit : 'in them'. 23 Cf. Prov. 23. 12. 24 Cf. Prov. 22. 19. 25 Cf. Prov. 4. 25. 26 Prov. 17. 27. 27 Prov. 18. 6. 28 Eph. 5. 17. 29 Cf. Jer. 6. 16. 30 Jam. 3. 5. 31 Jam. 3. 5-6. 32 Jam. 3. 6. 33 Jam. 3. 8-9. 34 Jam. 3. 10. 35 Jam. 3. 11. 36 Cf. Jam. 3. 12.

or the earth and the inhabited world. And by his word the heavens were established, and all their hosts by the breath of his mouth[37]. **5.** They did not escape their bounds, and the sun, the moon, and the stars did not change from the way which he ordained for them, but they perform their service by giving light to the whole creation. **6.** We, on the other hand, miserable, wretched, sinful men that we are, turn and escape from our bounds, and forsake the law of God and his commandments which he laid upon us, irreverently and shamelessly transgressing them, **7.** as it is written, 'Because of your hardness and your impenitent heart you treasure up for yourself wrath in the day of wrath and the revelation of the just judgement of God, who will render to every man according to his works'[38].

V. **1.** For this reason then be vigilant, and turn away from these feuds and quarrels, for they are useless and trivial. **2.** They are harmful * and destructive for the souls of those who desire their * p. 99
salvation and who love God and our Lord Jesus who gave himself a ransom for everyone[39] and died for us, that he might redeem us from all lawlessness, and purify us for himself a people specially his own[40], zealous for good works[41] which God has prepared in order that we should walk in them[42]. **3.** Therefore strive with yourself before you die, and watch over your struggle with yourself so as not to invalidate it before the hour comes when the soul of everyone will be plucked out from him. For thus it has been said,

[37] Ps. 32. 6. [38] Rom. 2. 5-6. [39] Cf. I Tim. 2. 6. [40] **ⲦⲞⲨⲎⲦ** stands for the N.T. Greek περιούσιος, for the meaning of which cf. G. KITTEL, *Theologisches Wörterbuch zum Neuen Testament*, Stuttgart, 1933 ff., VI, pp. 57 f.

The Coptic form **ⲦⲞⲨⲎⲦ** presents difficulties. According to CRUM, *Dictionary*, p. 447 b, it is the qual. of **ⲦⲞⲞⲨⲦⲈ** 'to gather', 'to collect', or perhaps of **ⲦⲞⲨⲞ** (p. 443 b) 'to show', 'to teach', 'to send'.

The ancient Egyptian equivalent of **ⲦⲞⲞⲨⲦⲈ** is *twt*. But two more ancient Egyptian words of the same form *(twt)* are relevant : 1) 'to be like', 'to be similar', 'to correspond'; hence, 'to be fit', 'to be meet', 'to be due', 'to be suited to', (cf. the Coptic noun **ⲦⲞⲨⲰⲦ** 'idol'). 2) 'to be perfect', 'to be beautiful', 'to be completely equipped', 'to be provided with'. The fact that **ⲦⲞⲨⲎⲦ** is paraphrased in Crum's examples by **ⲤⲞⲦⲠ, ⲦⲀⲈⲒⲎⲨ, ⲤⲈⲂⲦⲰⲦ, ⲤⲘⲞⲚⲦ**, may be an indication that this qual. form is a relic of one of the old words *twt* or a conflation of them.

(For the ancient Egyptian material, I am indebted to Dr. M. F. Laming Macadam). [41] Tit. 2. 14. [42] Cf. Eph. 2. 10.

'Prepare your works for the way'[43], which means, prepare your works for your departure out of the body. **4.** The Lord will give to you the chance, yea to all of us together, to depart from the evil and do the good[44] before the time comes, for it is a sentence, completing and cutting short, which God will execute upon the earth[45]. **5.** For he will judge the world in righteousness and the people in uprightness[46], those who have done good things unto a resurrection of life, those who have done evil things unto a resurrection of judgement[47].

[Fragment 30] *TO HERAI*

Besa the most humble writes to Herai.

I. **1.** Truly, according to the word of the apostle, I marvel that you so quickly turn from him who called you in the grace of Jesus Christ[1] unto a good hope to be a firstfruit of God, and how you have given place to the devil that he might turn you speedily from the good thought unto the evil thought, and from constancy to the attitude of disaffection, and from love and peace to hatred and quarrelling. **2.** Do you not know that Satan is a hater of good, always envying those who desire their salvation? **3.** For on this said our holy father, Apa Antonius, who knew the wickednesses of the enemy who hates those who love God, those who advanced
* p. 100 to him with all their heart[2], 'Truly, * my beloved, our carelessness and our humiliation and our perversion have not been injurious to us alone, but they have also been painful to the angels and to all the saints in Christ Jesus. **4.** Truly also, my sons, our humiliation grieves them all, whereas our salvation and our glory give joy and rest to them all. Therefore indeed they go round seeking us always, as it is written, "The angel of the Lord surrounds those who fear him and delivers them"'[3]. **5.** Again he says[4], 'But I shall tell you another thing that touches man from his beginning.

[43] Prov. 24. 42. [44] Cf. Ps. 36. 27. [45] Rom. 9. 28. [46] Cf. Ps. 9. 9. [47] Jn. 5. 29.

[1] Cf. Gal. 1. 6. [2] For the following quotation, cf. MIGNE, *P.G.* 40, 986 D f. For this and the two subsequent quotations from Antony, cf. also G. GARITTE, 'A propos des lettres de S. Antoine l'Ermite', *Le Muséon*, LII, pp. 11 ff. [3] Ps. 33. 8. [4] For the following quotation, cf. MIGNE, *P.G.* 40, 1050 D f.

If man advances to God to serve him with all his heart, God gives him great power and great joy so that every work of God is sweeter to him than honey and the honeycomb [5], and all the pains of the body are sweet to him, and the recitations and vigils and the whole yoke of godliness are sweet to him. **6.** But afterwards he is tested by these things, so that coldness for warmth, heaviness for lightness, grief and weariness for joy, hatred for love, bitterness for sweetness — all these things come upon the man that seeks after God until he [6] helps him and he [7] overcomes them. **7.** And when he overcomes them, the Spirit of God is always with him, giving him power not to fear again any evil thing [8], or contempt of man, or fear of demon'. **8.** For this has been said, 'Be sober and vigilant, because your adversary the devil goes, roaring as the lions, seeking to devour your souls' [9].

II. **1.** Thus also said the good abbot, Apa Antonius [10], 'Truly my sons, they [11] always bear ill will towards you in their wicked counsel, and their secret persecution and their subtle evils and their spirits that lead astray, and their blasphemous thoughts and their unbeliefs which they sow in our heart daily, and their hardenings of heart and their perplexities, and their * many sorrows * p. 101
which they bring upon us always, and their despondencies with which they cause our heart to be plagued daily, and all their rages and their calumnies which they teach us one towards another, and their self-justification in what is done, and their condemnation which they cast into our heart. **2.** And while we are alone, they make us sit in judgement on one another even in their absence from us. With their slanders which they arrogantly put [12] into our hearts, we are hard of heart and we decry one another, we are boastful to each other with our hard words, we are always troubled at heart, we blame one another and not ourselves, we think that our trouble comes through our [13] neighbours, we are

[5] Cf. Ps. 18. 11. [6] I.e. God. [7] I.e. the man that seeks after God. [8] Here our text ceases to correspond to that of Migne, but it is impossible to say where the quotation ended for Besa — here, after 'demon', or at the end of I Pet. 5. 8. [9] I Pet. 5. 8. [10] For the following quotation, cf. Migne, *P.G.* 40, 983 B ff., and also 40, 1012 B ff. Part of this quotation occurs also on p. 93. [11] I.e. demons. [12] The quotation on p. 93 has : 'plant'. [13] Lit. : 'your'. I have here adopted the reading of the quotation on p. 93.

judges of appearances while the arch-robber is inside the house; with quarrels and factions we fight each other [14], until we carry our point, in order that we may appear justified before each other. **3.** They incite us to things which we cannot do, and at the wrong time. They cause us to be weary of our lot, which is in fact profitable for us. So they also make us laugh when it is time to weep, and weep when it is time to laugh. **4.** In short, they always turn us away from the straight path with many other deceptions by which they make us their slaves, and all of which it is not now the time to reveal. But whenever they fill our heart with these things and we feed on them and they provide sustenance for us, then God is angry with us. **5**. Therefore do not be remiss in craving the goodness of the Father; perhaps help for you will come from him, that you may teach yourselves to know what is in truth fitting'.

III. **1**. So on no account let the enemy destroy your good purpose in which you advanced towards God, but be firm and do not alter, as it was said, 'For we have become partakers of Christ if we hold fast the beginning of the confidence firm unto the end' [15]. **2.** 'For in your constancy', said the Lord, 'you shall win your souls' [16]. And
* p. 102 * again, 'He who will endure to the end, he shall be saved' [17]. **3.** And again, encouraging all men and assuring them, he says, 'Remember Lot's wife' [18]. Do not turn back like her who turned back and became a pillar of salt [19], so that all might take a lesson from her. It was not said that she became a pillar of stone, but a pillar of salt, since salt is seasoned, that all those who know and understand may give heed to what happened to her. Do not therefore turn back like her, and endanger that which you began. **4.** Are you persuaded and do you wish that your name should be blotted out of the book of life [20] after it has been written, after you have been numbered with the saints and counted among the host of heaven, though you have been promised in faith and have known the Lord? **5.** Accordingly take courage, do not weakly turn back, for it has been said, 'The man who wishes to part from his friends seeks an excuse' [21]. **6.** And do not be like those who fell upon the rock and

[14] The quotation on p. 94 adds: 'in them'. [15] Heb. 3. 14. [16] Cf. Lk. 21. 19.
[17] Mt. 10. 22, Mt. 24. 13, Mk. 13. 13. [18] Lk. 17. 32. [19] Cf. Gen. 19. 26.
[20] Cf. Ps. 68. 29. [21] Prov. 18. 1.

immediately sprouted because there was not much earth under them, and who were scorched when the sun rose and withered because they had neither root nor moisture[22]; that is to say they immediately believe for a while, but in a time of temptation they turn away[23], as the Lord said. **7.** But lay hold on the good and be vigilant like those who fell on the good ground and bore fruit in constancy a hundredfold[24].

IV. **1.** For if you turn back, many of those who hate you will exult over you and mock you, and many of us, too, who fear God and desire your honour, position, and establishment, will sorrow and grieve. **2.** For thus the Lord said, 'Who amongst you, wishing to build a tower, will not first sit down and count its cost, to see whether he has enough to complete it, lest he lay the foundation and be unable to complete it, and all who see him mock him saying, "This man started building but was not able to complete it"?'[25] **3.** Truly, * the Lord Jesus Christ does not teach us to build a tower (* p. 103) but rather teaches us to direct our way and our heart towards heaven, as he said, 'No one can put his hand on the plough and, looking back, be fit for the kingdom of God'[26], and by this saying he tells us not to turn back from our constancy. **4.** Therefore do not let us be foolish, but know what the will of the Lord is[27] and hate the evil which is disaffection, and love the good[28] which is constancy perfected, as it has been said, 'And let constancy have a perfect work'[29].

V. **1.** So then I am concerned for you, and I counsel you not to behave remissly in tribulation, for therein our progress lies. It has been said, 'Our salvation is in time of tribulation'[30]. **2.** For if they despise you and you bear it as the Lord bore it when they despised him and mocked him, all the more will you receive honour and glory from God and men. **3.** As he said with his truthful mouth, 'Bless them that curse you, pray for them that persecute you'[31], and, 'He who will smite you on your cheek, to him turn your other one'[32]. **4.** Concerning you, too, I am indeed grieved, for I do not wish you to forfeit your soul, which the whole world

22 Cf. Mt. 13. 5-6 and Lk. 8. 6. 23 Cf. Lk. 8. 13. 24 Cf. Lk. 8. 15. 25 Lk. 14. 28-30. 26 Lk. 9. 62. 27 Cf. Eph. 5. 17. 28 Cf. Amos 5. 15. 29 Jam. 1. 4. 30 Is. 33. 2. 31 Lk. 6. 28. 32 Lk. 6. 29.

is not worth[33], or to be overcome by words of man, or for your good behaviour to be destroyed because occasion has been found for unprofitable talk, as it is written, 'Evil communications corrupt good manners'[34]. **5.** For these things are dust, and they are nothing in the sight of those who love God and his Christ, who, when he was cursed, did not curse, and when he suffered, was not provoked[35]. **6.** For us it is fitting that we should be like him who has set us an example in order that we may follow his ways[36] and be fellow-heirs and partners[37] with him in the kingdom of heaven.

VI. **1.** Therefore, strive with yourself before a time comes when each one shall break his heart saying, 'Why did I not want them * p. 104 * to teach me, and my heart turn away from reproofs?'[38] **2.** You remember what was said concerning the saints, 'They saw the promises which are in the kingdom of God. They confessed saying, "We are strangers and sojourners on the earth"[39]. **3.** For they who say such things make it manifest that they seek a city, and if they remembered the one they came from, they would have opportunity to return to it. But now they wish for the better one, that is to say the heavenly. Therefore God is not ashamed for them to invoke him as God over them. For he has prepared a city for them'[40]. **4.** You yourself remember these things. Do not go back on your promise which you made like those concerning whom it was said, 'They were stoned, they were sawn apart, they died by the sword[41]; they were tortured, they did not accept the deliverance of their body, that they might receive the more excellent resurrection'[42]. **5.** What does 'they did not accept the deliverance of their body' mean, unless that they did not wish to turn to the works of worldliness, but wished to turn away and be with God? **6.** The Lord will give you strength and will confirm you in every good work[43], that you may excel in the work of the Lord always. You know that in the Lord your suffering is not vain[44].

[33] Cf. Mt. 16. 26, Mk. 8. 36, Heb. 11. 38. [34] I Cor. 15. 33. [35] I Pet. 2. 23. [36] Cf. I Pet. 2. 21. [37] Cf. perhaps Eph. 3. 6. [38] Prov. 5. 12. [39] Cf. Heb. 11. 13. [40] Heb. 11. 14-16. [41] Heb. 11. 37. [42] Heb. 11. 35. [43] Cf. II Thes. 2. 17. [44] Cf. I Cor. 15. 58.

[Fragment 31]

ON THOSE WHO HAVE RENOUNCED THEIR CONSTANCY

Besa the most humble on those who have renounced their constancy by leaving us.

I. **1.** Our holy fathers since the day when they gathered together these monasteries have not sent for a man to make him a monk by force, nor have they compelled any man in the matter of[1] his property, nor have we ourselves done so either. **2.** For they used not to compel man to virtue, but our fathers appointed laws for us in their communities concerning our confirmation and concerning the establishment of the brethren, in order that they might be free from care and find means of serving the Lord in propriety and in attendance upon the Lord honourably without anxiety[2], as it is written, 'All things belonged to them in common, and there was not * one who said of the things which he had that they were * p. 105
his own'[3]. **3.** And our fathers laid it down for us in this manner, namely that[4] whoever comes in to be a monk with us shall from the first renounce everything which he has and make it over to the fellowship of God and the service of the poor; and that neither he nor any man related to him shall be able to go back and ask for anything, inasmuch as each one has pledged his word. **4.** Not only do all the brethren, from the least to the greatest, always subscribe in that way, but also our fathers who laid the foundation of these monasteries themselves began by subscribing thus. Moreover our fathers have written, 'If I want to depart, I shall gird myself with a cowl[5] and go : I shall not be able to go back and ask for anything'. **5.** This is the holy fellowship, where no one from the greatest to the least takes his ease and neglects another, but the same equality is for them all together, from the father who is in charge down to the very humblest — indeed the humblest are taken greater care of. **6.** These now who have renounced their constancy and oppose God have themselves, since the day they came to become monks, known the law laid down for us. Yet they do

[1] Or : 'on account of'. [2] Cf. I Cor. 7. 35. [3] Cf. Acts 4. 32. [4] For similar regulations, cf. J. Leipoldt, *Sinuthii archimandritae vita et opera omnia,* Paris, CSCO, 73/Copt.5 (1913), p. 71. [5] Meaning doubtful, cf. Crum, *Dictionary,* p. 312 b; possibly an apron or some other part of the monks' dress.

not obey it. Who compelled them? Why did they not depart to the place whence they had come before renouncing and resigning (their belongings)? **7.** For the laws of the churches and the laws of the monasteries are accounted to be quite inflexible especially for the common life. **8.** Therefore our fathers received another divine law concerning this matter, namely that whosoever has given up his belongings, whether by written or unwritten agreement, shall not return and ask for them, lest he cause the brethren hardship. These are commandments of life which cannot be undone.

[Fragment 32] *TO HERAI*

Besa writes to Herai who has broken the pledge of her constancy and forsaken the fountain of living water and dug for herself broken cisterns which will not be able to hold water [1].

I. **1.** Since you have chosen for yourself death rather than life [2], despised and abominated daughter, loved the curse rather * p. 106 * than the blessing [3], and loved the darkness rather than the light [4], and also reckoned the bitter sweet and the sweet bitter [5], **2.** they shall rightly say of you, 'Get down, sit on the ground, virgin daughter of Babylon, sit in your dishonour, Babylon, daughter of the Chaldeans. You shall not again be called tender and soft [6]. **3.** Uncover your veil, uncover your grey hairs, uncover the shins, cross the rivers. Your shame shall be revealed, your reproaches shall be manifest. I shall exact from you what is just. From henceforth I will not hand you over to man [7] to teach you. Sit you in grief, go into the darkness, daughter of the Chaldeans: you shall no longer be called the power of the kingdom [8]. **4.** Forasmuch as you loved the curse, it came upon you; you did not desire the blessing, it fled from you, and you put on the curse like a garment. It went like water into your bowels and like oil into your bones [9]. **5.** For the monastery into which you were received and where they gave you glory you insulted, saying, 'Your convent is the heavenly Jerusalem'. Truly it is the heavenly Jerusalem, and it is the mount God blessed. **6.** But you God has despised and

1 Cf. Jer. 2. 13. 2 Cf. Jer. 8. 3, Deut. 30. 19. 3 Cf. Ps. 108. 17, Deut. 30. 19. 4 Cf. Jn. 3. 19. 5 Cf. Is. 5. 20. 6 Is. 47. 1. 7 Is. 47. 2-3. 8 Is. 47. 5. 9 Cf. Ps. 108. 17-18.

condemned. He hated you alone out of all the holy and godfearing sisters who are in his holy monasteries, the monastery which you insulted in your arrogance and boastfulness, deceitful and rebellious daughter and daughter of Judas the traitor [10]. For you have said, 'I and no one else' [11].

II. **1.** For this reason destruction is coming upon you unawares [12], and widowhood and childlessness are coming upon you suddenly in your witchcraft and the power of your magic spells exceedingly, for the confidence in your wickedness [13]. **2.** Know that your contempt and your fornication shall become your shame, because you, like a lion in the forest, opened your mouth, and insulted the holy monastery of God. That is why he has hated you and cast you out of his holy monastery, even as he said, 'I will cast them out of my house, I will not love them any more' [14]. **3.** For you turned judgement into gall, and the fruit * of righteousness into bitterness [15], because your heart was corrupted, for you counted darkness for light and light for darkness [16]. Thus, therefore, you sowed wheat and reaped thorns [17]. For inasmuch as you loved the evil you hated the good [18]. So God has overthrown you utterly, he has plucked you up, he has removed you from your dwelling, and your root from the land of the living. **4.** The righteous who fear Christ will see you and say, 'Behold, a woman who did not make God her helper, but hoped on the abundance of her arrogance and her self-sufficiency' [19], even as it was said, 'In all these things foolish [20] Judah did not turn to me with all her heart, but to falsehood' [21]. **5.** Your disobedience will teach you and your wickedness will upbraid you. Know and see that it is bitter for you to forsake the Lord God [22]. For you think that if you are away from me you will profit. **6.** You have loved those who sleep with you [23] who are the demons, you have multiplied your fornication with them [24] in your darkened heart and your deceitful thoughts, and you have placed your remembrances behind the posts of your door [25] until you

* p. 107

10 Cf. Lk. 6. 16. 11 Is. 47. 8, Is. 47. 10. 12 Is. 47. 11. 13 Is. 47. 9-10. 14 Hos. 9. 15. 15 Cf. Amos 6. 12. 16 Cf. Is. 5. 20. 17 Cf. Jer. 12. 13. 18 Cf. Ps. 51. 5, Mic. 3. 2. 19 Cf. Ps. 51. 7-9. 20 The LXX reads : ἀσύνθετος. Our reading may have arisen out of a confusion between ἀσύνθετος and ἀσύνετος. 21 Jer. 3. 10. 22 Cf. Jer. 2. 19. 23 Is. 57. 8. 24 Is. 57. 9. 25 Is. 57. 8.

return to the salty earth out of which you were taken : for you are earth and to earth you have returned[26].

III. **1.** Though you came in uprightness, you did not finish in uprightness. Rather you came in deceit and also departed in falsehood. **2.** Therefore the curse shall devour you and neither root nor branch shall be left of you[27]. You came in vanity and in vanity you departed, so your name shall be covered in darkness[28], for you yourself are darkness in all your affairs, and shame shall cover you, because you have forsaken the commandment and have chosen destruction for yourself. **3.** For you did not know and you did not understand that God is not mocked[29] nor is he despised. Rather it is he who has mocked you, and it is you he has despised like flowing water. **4.** Therefore, even as the shame of a thief when arrested, * p. 108 * so were you ashamed at being caught because you rejected the word of God[30], and as the Lord said concerning the bloody city, 'Pass judgement against her and make manifest to her all her iniquities'[31], so also they shall pass judgement against you, or on you, and reveal to you all your iniquities, saying, 'O city that sheds blood in her midst, that her time may come'[32].

IV. **1.** For you have become an offence and a stumbling-block to those who advanced towards God, as it is written, 'He who will offend one of these little ones who believe in me, it is better for him that a millstone should be tied to his neck and he be sunk in the depth of the sea[33] rather than that he should offend one of these little ones who believe in me'[34]. **2.** This refers to you, for you have become a stumbling to many and have formed such desires as go against you and make you defiled in the blood you have shed. For you have fallen by the way, and in the deeds you have been doing you have been unclean. You have caused the days to approach, you have brought on the time of your years. **3.** So the Lord has made you to be a reproach and a jest both for those who are near to you and those who are far from you, you who are notoriously foul and abounding in iniquities[35]. It has also been said, as a threat, ' "You have perfected the end of your wickedness in violence, but me you have forgotten", says the Lord. "If I clap my hands together over

[26] Cf. Gen. 3. 19. [27] Cf. Mal. 4. 1. [28] Cf. Eccles. 6. 4. [29] Cf. Gal. 6. 7. [30] Cf. Jer. 8. 9. [31] Cf. Ez. 22. 2. [32] Ez. 22. 3. [33] Mt. 18. 6. [34] Cf. Lk. 17. 2. [35] Cf. Ez. 22. 3-5.

the things which I shall bring upon you for what you have done [36], will your heart endure or your hands be able to prevail on the day on which I shall do these things to you? I, the Lord, have spoken and will do it"' [37]. **4.** And you shall be desolate [38] because you have forsaken God, your saviour, and have not remembered your Lord. Therefore you shall plant an unfaithful plant and an unbelieving seed, and you shall go astray on the day when you shall plant it [39]. **5.** Again, 'Woe to you because you turned away from me. Misery shall overtake you because you did iniquity against me' [40], and, 'Your ways and your works did these things to you; this is your wickedness, for it is bitter, because it reached unto your heart' [41]. **6.** Again it is * said, 'Because you forgot me and put me behind your body [42] I will cast you away, my eye will not spare you, and I will have no mercy on you' [43]. * p. 109

V. **1.** Listen again to your disgrace and shame. It has been said, 'I planted you as a vine wholly bearing true fruit. How did you turn to bitterness, vine that became strange?' [44] **2.** For it were better for you that you had not come into the communities of the Lord than that you should have denied your constancy and the holy commandment which was given to you. For you have fallen upon your face like your father Judas the traitor, you have burst asunder and all your bowels have gushed out [45], because you are deceitful like that man. **3.** For if you had remembered how you would be punished in hell and if you had remembered the resting-places which are in the kingdom of heaven, you would not have been quite so contemptuous as to betray your constancy and the promise which you made. **4.** Repudiator of your pledges and denouncer of those who took you in, you are defiled in your blood. Your father is an Amorite and your mother a Hittite. As for your birth — on the day on which you were born, they did not bind your breasts or wash you with water or salt you with salt, and they did not wrap you in swaddling-clothes [46]. **5.** This means that you were never taught virtue, you did not know the commandment, and you were not taught to beware of evil. The Lord Jesus had no pity on you to do any of these things for you and have mercy

36 Ez. 22. 12-13. 37 Ez. 22. 14. 38 Cf. Is. 17. 9. 39 Is. 17. 10-11. 40 Cf. Hos. 7. 13. 41 Jer. 4. 18. 42 Ez. 23. 35. 43 Ez. 5. 11. 44 Jer. 2. 21. 45 Cf. Acts 1. 18. 46 Ez. 16. 3-4.

on you. But he came upon you and saw you defiled in your blood, and said to you, 'Out of your blood, increase in life'. 6. You were naked and unseemly and God remembered you in your humiliation and your iniquities. He spread out his wings over you, he covered your unseemliness, and he swore to you, he entered into a covenant with you, and you became his. He washed you with water, and he washed your blood from you, and he anointed you with oil[47]. **7.** That is to say he received you to himself in his loving-kindness, he taught you in his goodness, and he spread out his mercy upon you in his pity that you might perhaps be set right and fear the * p. 110 Lord. But you rejected all these things, * you feebly turned back and you denied your constancy.

VI. **1.** So he will say to you in anger and wrath, 'Therefore you shall not enter, nor shall it be so[48], because there have been perverse works in you, and you did not call to mind your infancy, the day when you were naked and unseemly and lived defiled in your blood'[49]. **2.** So therefore it shall be said concerning you as you deserve, 'O forsaker of the straight ways, who chooses for herself the ways of darkness[50], who takes pleasure in them that do evil and who rejoices at the wicked, whose ways are twisted, and whose paths are so devious that you become remote and estrange yourself from the purpose of the righteous'[51]. **3.** And again it shall be said concerning you, 'When I called you, you did not hear me. I spread abroad my words : you paid no heed. But you rejected my words and you disobeyed my upbraidings. Therefore, I will also mock at your perdition and I will deride you when perdition comes upon you, when trouble befalls you suddenly and overthrow comes upon you like a whirlwind, when perdition comes upon you, and when tribulation comes to you and you are in straits[52]. **4.** It shall come to pass that you call upon God and he will not hear you, for you have hated wisdom and have not chosen for yourself the love of God. You preferred not to pay heed to the counsels of God and sneered at his upbraidings. Therefore you shall eat the fruits of

[47] Cf. Ez. 16. 5-9. [48] Cf. Ez. 16. 8. The passage may therefore be paraphrased : 'you shall not enter into a covenant with me'. The second phrase may also be dependent on Ez. 16. 8 and therefore mean : 'nor shall she (you) become mine'. [49] Ez. 16. 22. [50] Cf. Prov. 2. 13. [51] Prov. 2. 14-16. [52] Cf. p. 12, n. 16.

your way of life and be filled with your own iniquities' [53]. For you did not believe God or hope for his salvation which he wrought with you.

VII. **1.** Therefore this lament shall be spoken over you, 'This foolish virgin stumbled, she fell, she shall no more rise. She stumbled, she fell upon the earth and there shall be no one to help her' [54]. **2.** For you hated the reproofs at the gates [55], which are the house of God, and you obliterated the holy words. You entered openly in the light of the day, but you passed over by another side in the night like a thief and a robber [56] to despoil yourself. **3.** So God * will uncover the things appertaining to your hinder parts and * p. 111
bring them before you, that your shame may be revealed and the strangeness of your fornication, your iniquity, and your clamour [57]; and also because you impertinently stood up to demand that which you had given the Lord God, having promised it for your soul, because the fear of God is far from you and you took no thought for your end. **4.** So, as it was said, 'Samaria shall be destroyed because she stood up against her God' [58], and you too shall be destroyed and you shall not obtain salvation, because you have stood up against your God, you have departed from him in your impudence, since the snare of the hunter, that is to say the devil, is upon all your ways [59], and you have turned your back and not your face to him. **5.** For you did not consider nor did you reflect that the things you promised to God were from then on no longer yours but God's. **6.** So if you were to withdraw some of these things, you would not be like people taking their [60] own goods, but you would resemble those who rob the temple of the Lord. And this thing, namely the promise, did not extend to belongings only, but even to words and intentions. Now you have promised, and the promises are binding, so you must keep them. Instead [61], you have begged to be let off all these things.

VIII. **1.** Will you not suffer the lesson which Ananias and Sapphira [62] suffered when they promised the price of the property, but stole some of what they had promised, so that an evil death

[53] Cf. Prov. 1. 24-31. [54] Cf. Amos. 5. 1-2. [55] Cf. Amos 5. 10. [56] Cf. Jn. 10. 1. [57] Cf. Jer. 13. 26-27. — ϩⲙ̄ϩⲙ̄ lit. : 'roaring', 'neighing'. [58] Hos. 14. 1. [59] Cf. Hos. 9. 8. [60] Lit. : 'your' (fem. sg.). [61] Lit. : 'behold'. [62] Cf. Acts 5. 1 ff.

shortly overtook those transgressors? **2.** If you had not promised, there would have been no sin to your charge, but inasmuch as you made a promise and went back on it, therefore your sin is great and it is hard for God to forgive you. As the Lord said to his disciples, 'It is easier for a camel to go through the eye of a needle than for a rich man to enter the kingdom of God'[63]. **3.** Moreover, as a woman rejects her husband, so you have rejected the covenant which you established with God, because you are a perverse woman, provoking to anger, whose spirit has not trusted in God. For you * p. 112 have neglected * the covenant of the Lord, and you did not want to walk in his ways, but you have turned away quickly from the way which you agreed to before the Lord Jesus. **4.** Do not think that I say these things hating you, but truly I am grieved at the hardness of heart which has come over you. Really, this is your own injury, and it has come upon you because the light grew dark in you until you denied your constancy and forsook God, your saviour. **5.** Consequently it was said concerning you thus, 'You wearied yourself and yet did not say, "I will now stop being strong because I did these things"[64]. Therefore, you did not remember me and you did not put me in your thoughts or in your heart. I also, when I see you, will ignore you, and you feared me not. I also shall proclaim my righteousness and your wickednesses which shall not profit you. If you cry unto them, let them deliver you from your tribulation. All these the wind shall take and a whirlwind shall scatter'[65]. **6.** For you have forgotten God who saves you, who brought you out of the iron furnace[66], which is the world, and you have turned thither, and to it again, that you might go down into the clay mixed with chaff and seize the brick, and a fire might devour you there[67]. For who ... *1 folio missing* ...

[Fragment 33]

BESA'S DEFENCE AGAINST UNJUST ACCUSATIONS

I. **1.** says, 'For every creature shall be arraigned for judgement concerning everything that was overlooked, be it good or bad'[1].

63 Mt. 19. 24, cf. Mk. 10. 25, Lk. 18. 25. 64 Is. 57. 10. 65 Is. 57. 11-13.
66 Cf. Deut. 4. 20, III Kg. 8. 51, Jer. 11. 4. 67 Cf. Nah. 3. 14-15.
1 Eccles. 12. 14.

2. 'Let our eyes', according to the scriptures, 'look at things that are upright and our eyelids open wide to the truths'[2]. 'Vanity of vanities it is', says the preacher, 'everything that is in them is vanity'[3]. **3.** Do not think, brethren and men such as they are, that we have kept this little one until to-day because of things that will perish, or because of matters such as we have heard that many have said. **4.** I tell you, and I declare before God and our Lord Jesus, that there is no such thing in my heart; but I fear * God for the little innocent's sake lest he be dragged to perdition, and lest sin before God be on our heads because we neglected a sinless soul; and we say that when he learns wisdom and knows good and evil, he is responsible, and there shall be no sin. He was given to God, and for that reason we have striven for him. **5.** But restless and wicked men who have progressed in evil, who err and who lead others astray[4], are responsible because they have seized him by force against the will of God and against our will. Their blood is upon their head and their iniquity is coming down upon their pate[5]. **6.** For we are all coming into the hands of God[6] and each one shall give account for what he does[7]. They have despised us and insulted the brethren. **7.** Let us indeed be worthy that they should despise us for the sake of God's name and for Christ, for because of his name we have suffered. They despised God and crucified him unto death and his holy apostles and all our fathers who bore reproaches because of his name.

* p. 113

II. **1.** But as for people who plot evil things against the monasteries of God, and who slanderously and blasphemously say against his communities, 'You have put men to death', (I say) neither we nor our blessed fathers ever killed a man, nor do we know of such a thing. But the real murderers are plain to see. **2.** So they who say these things shall be cursed in all their works before God, because they have lied about his holy monasteries. **3.** For even thus has it been said, 'Be not silent, O God, and be not still, for, behold, your enemies have cried out and they who hate you have lifted up their heads. They have taken evil counsel against your people, and schemed against your saints'[8]. **4.** Thus also it has been said in rebuke, 'O God, be not silent concerning my

[2] Cf. Prov. 4. 25. [3] Eccles. 12. 8. [4] Cf. II Tim. 3. 13. [5] Cf. Ps. 7. 17.
[6] Cf. Heb. 10. 31. [7] Cf. Rom. 14. 12. [8] Ps. 82. 2-4.

praise, for the mouths of the sinner and the deceitful have opened against me; they have spoken against me with a deceitful tongue. They compassed me with words of hatred and fought against me without a cause. Instead of loving me they slandered me, but I was praying. They set up for me evil for good and hatred for my
* p. 114 love'[9]. **5.** * So it was said in anger, 'Set the sinner against them and those who approve of them. Let the devil stand at their right hand. When they receive judgement let them come forth condemned. Let their prayer become sin unto them, and their days be few. Let their children be orphans and their wives widows[10] ...
2 folios missing ...

[Fragment 34] *CONTINUATION OF BESA'S DEFENCE*

I. **1**. the Lord in grief saying, 'Hear me, Lord, hear the voice of my justification. Do men repay evil for good? For they have spoken words against my soul, and they have hidden their punishment from me. Remember then the day when I stood before you speaking good things on their behalf, that you might turn your wrath from them. **2.** Therefore', it has been said, 'deliver up their sons to famine and gather them to the sword[1]. Let there be a cry in their houses; suddenly you shall bring robbers upon them, for they have undertaken the task of seizing me and have hidden snares for me. **3.** But you, Lord, have known all their counsel which they have taken against me even unto death. Do not cleanse their iniquities and do not blot out from before you the sins of their fathers. Let their infirmity come before you. You shall deal with them in the time of your anger'[2]. And not only this, but it was also said, 'Give them Lord : what will you give them? Give them a barren womb and dry breasts'[3]. **4.** But you, O holy brethren, partakers of the heavenly calling[4], we know your love. Even as you pray for my wretchedness — not only you but all others too — pray that we may recover from the infirmity. **5.** But these men, just as Judas betrayed the Lord, who was his life, when they covenanted with him to give him money[5], so now have these men done by grasping at money in order to kill us or maltreat us.

9 Ps. 108. 1-5. 10 Cf. Ps. 108. 6-9.

1 Jer. 18. 19-21. 2 Jer. 18. 22-23. 3 Hos. 9. 14. 4 Cf. Heb. 3. 1.
5 Cf. Lk. 22. 5.

II. **1.** Therefore, as it has been said, 'Cursed is the man who
puts his hope on man and sets the flesh * of his arm upon him and * p. 115
lets his heart turn away from the Lord. He shall be like a wild ass[6] in the desert. He shall not see good things when they come, but he shall be in dry places in the wilderness, in a salty, uninhabited land. **2.** But blessed is the man who trusts in the Lord, and whose hope the Lord shall be. He shall be like a tree flourishing by the water and he shall throw out his roots to moisture, and he shall not fear when heat comes upon him. Branches with many leaves shall be upon him, and he shall not fear if one year the rain does not come, and he shall not fail to bring forth fruit. His heart is a wonder beyond everything, and it is man. **3.** Who then is he that will know him? It is I, the Lord, who tries the hearts and proves the reins, to give to everyone according to his ways and according to the fruit of his works'[7]. **4.** Therefore, we are in the hands of God and his Christ, and our care is cast on him[8], that he may deliver us from every evil thing[9], and save us from restless and wicked men[10]. The Lord shall return to everyone his righteousness and his faithfulness[11]. **5.** But you, beloved brethren who fear God, pray you all that God may guard us from every evil and save us from this evil age[12] and the dangers of false brethren[13]. **6.** It is possible for us to tell you fully how those men acted, but now instead[14] we have desisted, giving place to God, and those men too, if their heart is to be at ease or if they are to have satisfaction, must settle it with God. **7.** I, according to my wretchedness, do not see any evil that I did to man. But it is written, 'He who shall recompense evil for good, evil will not stir from his house'[15].

Apa Besa.

[Fragment 35] *A DENUNCIATION OF AN ERRING NUN*

Or [who] shall [bemoan] you, or who shall turn to you in
peace? * Because you turned away from me', says the Lord, 'you * p. 116

[6] The LXX reads : ἀγριομυρίκη. [7] Jer. 17. 5-10. [8] Cf. perhaps I Pet. 5. 7. Alternatively the phrase could be translated : 'our concern is fixed on him'. [9] Cf. II Tim. 4. 18. [10] Cf. II Thes. 3. 2. [11] I Kg. 26. 23. [12] Cf. Gal. 1. 4. [13] Cf. II Cor. 11. 26. [14] Lit. : 'behold'. [15] Prov. 17. 13.

shall go backwards'[1]. ... For you have provoked God, the Christ, to anger on account of strangers, who received you to himself from the path of your lawlessness, and you have angered him with your abominations. [Or] did you not consider so as to know the things he has done for you. Right[ly] ... *Unknown number of lines missing* ... Salt is good, but if the salt is insipid wherewith shall it be seasoned?[2] It has been said, 'It is not useful for the land, nor for the dunghill, but it is cast out[3] and trodden on by all men'[4], simply as they are. Moreover it has been well said, 'Man being in honour did not understand, he was likened to ignorant beasts, he resembled them[5]. This is your way; it shall be a stumbling-block to you'[6]. How long... *Unknown number of lines missing* ... lift up your [eyes] towards uprightness and see where you have not been defiled. You have lain for them in your ways like a solitary crow, and you have defiled the land in your fornications and your evils[7]. You have acquired much contempt[8] for a stumbling-block for yourself. Yours has become a harlot's face. You have been shamed before everyone. Did you not call me as kinsman and as[9]... *The missing and fragmentary lines may have contained parts of Jer. 3. 4 and 3. 5* ... or shall this be for a victory for you. Behold, you have spoken and done all these wickednesses and you have waxed strong[10]. [Nevertheless] whether we, or you, or everyone together, we shall not delay to come into the hands of God and each one shall receive from his hand according to his works whether good or evil[11]. Even as also... *Unknown number of lines missing* ... [Let there not be for them he who] receives them to himself, let no one be merciful to his orphans. Let their children be blotted out and let their name be blotted out in a single generation[12]. And let the lawlessnesses of his fathers be remembered before [the Lord][13]. ... *The missing lines of text probably contained the remainder of Ps. 108.14 and 108.15.* ...
* p. 117 [Because they did not remember] to do mercy, they persecuted * the wretched and poor, and the broken-hearted to kill him. They loved

[1] Jer. 15. 5-6. [2] Lk. 14. 34. [3] Cf. Lk. 14. 35. [4] Cf. Mt. 5. 13. [5] Ps. 48. 13, Ps. 48. 21. [6] Cf. Ps. 48. 14. [7] Jer. 3. 2. [8] The LXX reads: ποιμήν; our reading may have arisen from a confusion between cωϣ and ϣωc. [9] Cf. Jer. 3. 3-4. [10] Cf. Jer. 3. 5. [11] Cf. II Cor. 5. 10. [12] Cf. Ps. 108. 12-13. [13] Ps. 108. 14.

the curse, [it came] upon them; [they did not] desire the [blessing], it shall flee from them. They put on the curse [like] a [garment], it went[14] ... *The missing lines of text probably contained the remainder of Ps. 108.18 and 108.19* ... always. This is the work of those who [slander] me [and] those who speak evils against my soul[15]. Do not ... I say ... *6 lines* ... to the name ... to this ... *Unknown number of lines missing* ... we shall also say as ... *1 line* ... their holy fathers, 'Who shall separate us from the love of God[16] which is in Christ Jesus, our Lord?

CODEX C

[Fragment 36] *ON INDIVIDUAL RESPONSIBILITY FOR SINS*

I. **1.** O foolish virgins and still more than you. But we never did that which the world does, be it in fornication, be it in honourable marriage, be it in a bed undefiled[1]. The Lord bears witness! For we are not commending ourselves[2] saying these things to you, but I say these things to you and I tell you that I am innocent of your condemnation. Your blood shall be upon you and upon your pate. **2.** Who amongst our fathers ever came to you from the beginning, having enjoined upon you a covenant from the Lord? Or on which day did our first father, [who has died], come to you, having spoken with you mouth to mouth for a testimony to you? **3.** Or when did [he] ever come to you having spoken with you thus, or our other reverend father who has not long * been dead, except concerning * p. 118
this only that he might come and appoint for you the offering and go forth and depart without seeing you? **4.** Therefore, not only am I innocent of your judgement, but also my holy and blessed fathers who have died are guiltless of your blood. And I have come from them that your blood may be upon your head. **5.** And not only this that they are innocent of your judgement, but also [our] reverend [father], Apa Pshoi, and all the elders are innocent of your judgement and they are guiltless of your blood. For he, for his part also, did not refrain from telling you the truth while coming

14 Cf. Ps. 108. 16-18. 15 Cf. Ps. 108. 20. 16 Rom. 8. 35.

1 Cf. Heb. 13. 4. 2 Cf. perhaps II Cor. 5. 12.

to you many times. **6.** Shenoute also and Papnoute are innocent of your blood. Moreover, all the other holy elders, who are with us and who are of one mind with us, are guiltless of your blood; and your menfolk and your brethren and your children and all those who are with us from our least to our greatest, all are innocent of the reproach which will come upon you at the time of your need. **7.** But you, brethren, who are holy and who suffer, your blessing is upon your head. The Lord shall bless you; the Lord shall guard you and all your sufferings. And you are innocent of the blood of every sinner amongst us, whether great or small; you yourselves are responsible[3]. But thus have I spoken with you inside the veil, upon the altar of the Lord, and you have transgressed the words which I have commanded in the presence of God. **8.** Therefore, behold, I shall stand and reprove you before the throne of the glory of God. And I shall reprove you, not being separated from you even as still in this world, nor being far from you but only a footstep away. **9.** Therefore, I tell you that I shall reprove you face to face before the Lord Jesus, who will require your blood from my hands. But I am innocent of your blood, because I have commanded you; and not only have I commanded, but also with strokes and upbraidings and entreaties and very many things which it is not at all fitting that I should do, so that I am like a wicked man before you, though I have nothing at all towards
* p. 119 you except the love of God. **10.** * And as I want it to be with me in the place to which I shall go, so also (I want) it to be with you, or more than with me, for I am not worthy of this. Furthermore, as I do not want it not to be with me in that place, so also (I do not want) it not to be with you.

II. **1.** Nevertheless, as I am far from you and not at all near to you in my heart, so also am I far from you in my soul. Are your blood and your condemnation upon us? And as I am not with you in the body, so also I prevent my spirit from abiding with you. But, indeed, I am not worthy of this, for I am a miserable sinner, yet my spirit is not in agreement with you. **2.** If, therefore, your least brother shall prevent his spirit from abiding with you, O miserable ones, then how much more shall the

[3] I.e. each one bears the responsibility for himself only.

Lord of all, Jesus, prevent his Holy Spirit from abiding with you, who says, 'My Spirit shall not dwell in these men for ever, because they are flesh'[4], and sensualists, boasters, which means you. **3.** But if you yourselves will not dwell in ruined and abandoned places where there are wild beasts, and where foxes, snakes, and scorpions breed, and where swine feed, then how shall the Spirit of Christ dwell in your ruined souls and your destroyed hearts and your bodies which are lairs of unclean spirits? **4.** Or how shall the spirits of the righteous and all the saints, whose words we read, repose with you, while demons breed with you and repose in your foul-minded thoughts, and nurture their wickednesses in your machinations and your defiled mind? **5.** If woe be to a scarer of men, as it is written, 'scarers of men'[5], then how much more is it woe to you, if you scare away from you the Spirit of the Lord. And how shall you be reckoned as the Lord's, if you scare it away from you? Is it not indeed written, 'He who has not the Spirit of the Lord is not his'[6]? **6.** And if you would not like to be shut up in the dark, then how shall the Spirit * of the Lord like to abide in your hearts which are dark, and your souls in which there is no light at all? **7.** If you would not ever call idols blessed which are set up in temples — sticks and stones with no spirit in them, but set fast with nails and other kinds of manufactured things, and when anyone moves them, they will collapse —, then which angel from God shall call you blessed, or which spirit of the prophets and the apostles will come and abide with you while the Spirit of the Lord is not with you, nor beside you? **8.** But you are set fast upon manufactured words and empty things, and when anyone moves you, you will collapse and be cast to the ground by the demons who deceive and mock you, whereas it is fitting that you should mock them. **9.** Or[7] do you not know that, as the Lord has said to his disciples, 'Into whatsoever house you shall enter, first say, "Peace to this house". And if there is a son of peace there, your peace shall rest upon it. But if not it shall return to you'[8], **10.** thus also the Lord is wont to say to the[9] Holy Spirit, "The place or the community into which you shall enter, if there is a

* p. 120

[4] Gen. 6. 3. [5] Cf. I Tim. 1. 10. — The Greek N.T. has : ἀνδραποδιστής.
[6] Cf. Rom. 8. 9. [7] Zoega CCXXXVI omits : 'or'. [8] Lk. 10. 5-6.
[9] Zoega CCXXXVI : 'his'.

son of peace there, or[10] therein, then[11] let your peace rest upon it and abide[12] with them. But if not, let it return to you and you return to heaven or the place wherein they shall be worthy of you'.

III. **1.** These things I say weeping, even as I have wept many times before to-day and still now, the Lord being witness. And also our[13] little brother who writes these words is witness, being thus troubled and weeping also, seeing me weep, my tears flowing over cheeks and down upon the ground[14], while I stand before
* p. 121 him often and he writes * not only what I say to him[15] now, but he also writes many other words. **2.** And[16] they were written three years before our reverend father died, when I spoke them weeping because of you, your sons, your daughters, your brethren, your folk, and because of myself also, and everyone who is with us together. **3.** And I was wanting at that time to tell you what we say, but I did not find the opportunity because of the jealousy of him who hates us, which is Satan. Afterwards[17] I came to you, walking[18] on foot, because it pleased the Lord of the whole earth[19]. I have not been commending myself[20], saying these things[21]. **4.** For[22] I myself am despised and greatly disgraced, but I tell you that your wretched brother — which means myself — is troubled at heart and has pity upon you. But you are not troubled at heart concerning yourselves nor again[23] do you have pity upon yourselves, O wretched ones, that no one among all the saints shall have pity upon you at the time of your need, at the time when the wheat shall be separated from the chaff[24], at the time when the sheep shall be separated from the goats[25], and when the net shall be drawn up and they collect the good into their vessels but cast the bad away[26].

10 Zoega CCXXXVI omits : 'there or'. 11 Zoega CCXXXVI omits : 'then'. 12 Zoega CCXXXVI : 'and you abide'. 13 Zoega CCXXXVI : 'your'. 14 Zoega CCXXXVI : 'flowing down over my cheeks, down upon the ground'. 15 Zoega CCXXXVI omits : 'to him'. 16 Zoega CCXXXVI omits : 'and'. 17 Zoega CCXXXVI adds : 'then'. 18 Zoega CCXXXVI omits : 'walking'. 19 Zoega CCXXXVI omits : 'of the whole earth'. 20 Cf. perhaps II Cor. 5. 12. 21 Zoega CCXXXVI adds : 'to you'. 22 Zoega CCXXXVI omits : 'for'. 23 Zoega CCXXXVI omits : 'again'. 24 Cf. Mt. 3. 12, Lk. 3. 17. 25 Cf. Mt. 25. 32. 26 Cf. Mt. 13. 48.

IV. **1.** I tell you I often weep until I can no longer, being greatly troubled in heart. For if you shall be separated from your children and your brethren and all your people in this dwelling-place and shall also be separated from them in unending eternity, then why did you separate from them? And if you shall not have the satisfaction of your children and your * brethren and your menfolk * p. 122 and all your people, then why did you depart from those who are of your kin? **2.** And if you shall not find the saints that you may be with them in heaven, and if you shall not find a resting-place, then why did you forsake them? And if you, gathered in these communities in heaven, shall not have the satisfaction of one another, then you are more wretched than all men, because you have not had the satisfaction of all those who belong to you in this world and you shall not make a feast for them[27] in the place to which you shall go. **3.** But if I, this wretched one, spend a single week without having seen your children and your brethren and your menfolk and all those who are with us together, I am looking forward to them like a brother who has not seen his brethren for a year; and (this is) out of my desire towards them and also their desire, which is more towards me than my desire is towards them. **4.** And so we, together, are greatly desirous of seeing one another hourly, daily, and every day, then who are you not to be desirous of seeing your children and your brethren in the place whither you shall go? **5.** Actually, I see you now, if you spend a single month without seeing them, you are upset concerning them and are wondering because you have not seen them, just as they too wish to see you, in order that we may repent of all our wickednesses together, and together perhaps become worthy of one another, and have our fill of mutual consolation, from the least to the greatest. **6.** If you, therefore, are desirous of seeing them in this dwelling-place and endure for God's sake, then how much more shall you be desirous of seeing them when you are separated from them in the place whither we[28] shall go, not because of God but because of our negligence and the obstinacy which has * overwhelmed * p. 123 the good thought, not letting it approach you so that you may not perceive it. **7.** And I was thinking that you would make the

27 BM 176 : 'and you shall not be worthy of them'. — This is probably the better reading. 28 BM 176 : 'you'.

feast of life[29] together, you, your children, your brethren, and your menfolk. But now I tell you that many of us shall be estranged from their own, and from their fathers, and their brethren, because they have not wanted to abase themselves, but surrendered themselves to pollution, to every uncleanness, because they did not take to themselves the fear of God. This means you.

V. **1.** Now, therefore, if you will not repent quickly — for the wrath of God has already burnt against you as it is written[30] For instead of being to us a comfort and a joy and an encouragement, you, on the other hand, because you are unoccupied with the concern for the wisdom of God, as it is written, 'There is wisdom in everyone who takes care'[31] for the things of righteousness to the establishment of an assembly by the Lord Jesus, you have now become a grief to us and an affliction and a heart-break. **2.** The Lord Jesus knows that because of the care for your children, and your brethren, and because of your care also, and the care of us all together, I have not gone to the place from which I came out since the first day of the great Passover. But I do not lose heart, knowing that he who will give my fathers' reward to them because they have nurtured us with teaching and have taken care of us with labour and trouble, with all understanding and every good work, will also give to me my little morsel of reward. **3.** Therefore, I shall again endeavour to take care of the work which God entrusted to me, and especially to take care of the poor. And it was[32] proper to think little of you in your bodily needs, but I will command the elder and all your brethren to take care of you in everything that you may not find an excuse to make[33]. But you are responsible. **4.** Your condemnation is not upon Shenoute nor Papnoute nor all the brethren who take care of you. Moreover, Jesus is guiltless of the affliction which is coming upon you at the
* p. 124 time * of your need. For I came to you on his behalf for a witness to them. **5.** And I did not come to you for a whim and a mockery and an idling, in the way that many are being deceived by such things, but I came to you and I spoke with you that the word of

29 Or more probably read : 'you would be worthy of life'. 30 Cf. O.T. passim. 31 Prov. 14. 23. 32 The addition : 'not' has been suggested as an emendation, cf. CRUM, *Dictionary*, p. 607 b, but I do not consider it necessary. 33 Lit. : 'word to say'.

the Lord might be accomplished, 'Your house is abandoned to you'[34], and also that the word of the apostle might be established, 'Your blood is on your head'[35]; and[36] in order that I may be innocent of your judgement, but[37] you yourselves responsible. 6. Nevertheless, as my fathers will judge me, so will I pass judgement on you in the place to which we shall go. For I have not forgotten to tell you the things which are advantageous to you[38].

[Fragment 37]

ON THE RESPONSIBILITIES OF THE SUPERIORS IN A CONVENT

I. **1.** Therefore, I tell you from God that I shall require your blood from the hands of her who is called mother with you and her who comes after her. And I shall require your blood from the hands of everyone to whom anyone is entrusted with you. And I shall require your blood, each from the other. And I shall require the blood of each one of you from her own hand, from the greatest to the least of you, and from her who is incapable to her who is capable of completing a task. **2.** If I am a debtor because I came to you once, or two or three times, having spoken with you by word of mouth, let me be judged by you in that place. And if you are debtors because I came to you and we made a covenant before the Lord Jesus who sits upon the throne of his glory[1] : **3.** for whether I am despised or honoured[2], it is necessary that I pass judgement * upon each one of you before him, because I did not refrain from * p. 125 coming to you and speaking with you by word of mouth. For it is necessary for you yourselves that each one of you receive according to her works before him. **4.** But is there indeed, in spite of the amount of negligence which misleads your spirit, such an idea in your hearts as to look at the face of the Lord Jesus and the face of all his saints or towards our fathers who have gathered you in that they may see you in joy? **5.** Now, instead, you are to us[3] a reproach and an affliction in heaven. For they departed from us, greatly afflicted concerning you, because your way is not towards

34 Mt. 23. 38. 35 Acts 18. 6. 36 Zoega CCXXXVI adds : 'also'. 37 Zoega CCXXXVI omits : 'but'. 38 Zoega CCXXXVI omits this sentence, and there is no indication, as there is in BM 175, that a new section is to begin.

1 Cf. Mt. 19. 28, Mt. 25. 31. 2 Zoega CCXXXVI adds : 'for'. 3 Zoega CCXXXVI : 'them'.

uprightness nor towards purity[4], as it is written. **6.** Or is it in your heart to see us even as we wish to see you? If so, why have you not paid heed to my word which I spoke to you by word of mouth, you all hearing, 'Do not hide anything among you from us, but communicate it to us that we may adjudge it either by means of your elders appointed for you or by all those belonging to you who are on the way to you'. **7.** Why are you hindered from telling us what goes on among you? Is it not inseparable (from the fact) that it is not borne in upon your minds that you should look upon your children, and your brethren, and your menfolk, and your fathers, and all those belonging to you and to all of us together, in the place where male is not separated from female, and in the place where our work and yours shall be made manifest as it is[5]; **8.** and in the place where the work of some shall be made manifest as being dark and they too shall be like it in darkness and gloom; and in the place where the work of others shall be light and they too shall be shining like the light[6], as it is written. **9.** Or again is it in your heart for each one of you to look upon the face of her neighbour in the place whither we shall go? If so, then why does
* p. 126 each one of you walk deceitfully? * You, on the one hand, say, 'I will not tell this one the evil which is in my heart against her'; and this other one says, 'I will not speak of my hatred which is in

CODEX D

[Fragment 38] *A CATECHESIS COMMEMORATING SHENOUTE*

A Catechesis of our holy father, Apa Besa, the archimandrite, which he pronounced on the day of the commemoration of our lord, the holy father, the prophet, Apa Shenoute, on the seventh day of the month Epeph[1]. With God's peace, amen.

I. **1.** May the Lord God Almighty bless you and your children. The love which is in you towards God is that which gathers you to this place and he to whom you are running is the Saviour Jesus. May the Saviour Jesus, therefore, now bless each one of you here to-day. **2.** If, where two or three are gathered together in his name,

[4] Cf. Jer. 4. 11. [5] Cf. I Cor. 3. 13. [6] Prov. 4. 18.

[1] I.e. July 1st.

the Lord is with them in their midst[2], how much more in this great multitude which is gathered to this holy place to-day in his name and in commemoration of his holy servant, Apa Shenoute. **3.** Truly, you are worthy to be remembered always, O my holy father. For the holy apostle, Paul, says, 'Remember your great ones who spoke to you the word of God; regarding the loftiness of their way of life, imitate their faith'[3]. **4.** You are honoured in your life and you are also honoured in your death and your name shall be blessed with us and with God. The saying of David is true, 'The righteous shall be for a memorial for ever'[4]. And, 'Your memorial shall be from generation to generation'[5]. **5.** We know the sufferings which you have sustained upon this mount. We know your love for the poor, and God does not forget your tears, your prayers, and your vigils. How shall anyone say of a man who has glorified God on earth that God, for his part, has not glorified him at his side? **6.** I say this : how shall he not repay the sufferings of a man who has been filled with the recitation of the scriptures and the pains * of Christ? Go up upon this rock * p. 127
and see the sufferings for us

CODEX E

[Fragment 39] *TO A NUN IN CHARGE IN A CONVENT*

rebellion against God and questioning and indifference, and how shall God not require of you people who are for him like his angels, whom he has entrusted to you. What do you think? Tell me especially the counsel which is in you that we may know whether it pleases the Lord. Wherein have I been profiting with you from the beginning because of your fair speech and flattery[1] in that you praise one another, being made to fall in your desires of heart and I also fall ... *(?) 5 lines* ... because of our wickednesses which we perpetrated at that time of which we are now ashamed, according to the word of the apostle, for the end of those wicked works is death[2], their obliteration by the wrath of God in those days.

2 Cf. Mt. 18. 20. 3 Heb. 13. 7. 4 Ps. 111. 6. 5 Cf. Ps. 134. 13, Ps. 101. 13.

1 Cf. Rom. 16. 18. 2 Cf. Rom. 6. 21.

But thanks be to Jesus that, even if he has increased his wrath, he has restrained us so as not to obliterate us. If we do not know with us and with you the grace of the Lord which he has wrought with us at this present time ... *(?) 2 lines* ... in all the [letters] from us being assembled together. And you too, if you do not discern for yourself, you will say that I hate you when I say these things to you thus. But I tell you that I remember your suffering and the others who are with you when I say these things to you. But know this : if you do not lay it to your heart from to-day on to cut off from yourself all ingratiating[3] and all hypocrisy, and speak the truth with the people entrusted to you and send to us a sound report and not to dissemble with ... *(?) 4 lines* ... into judgement, you and [they]. I shall grieve you and I shall withdraw from you little by little my heartfelt love which I have * p. 128 towards * you, for you are turning aside in this manner, and God hates me and is angry with me because I forbore with you before. Do you not cut off from the word of truth and the sound teaching the people with you whom Jesus will require of you? If the desire to please man were not dominating you rather than to please God, it[4] would not come ... *5 lines* ... There is a saying in the mouths of men : a son was given to a fool; he killed him with much kissing. Thus also, there are men to whom Jesus has entrusted people as sons and as daughters; they killed them with their fair speech and their flattery[5], forbearing with them in fleshly desires until they die in every wickedness, and they did not discipline them according to the scriptures with strokes and upbraidings that they might live in all goodness. And if you were ... *4 lines* ... and you too fall, you would not do anything lest you should grieve her that she should not grieve you also; but you urge on some who request things after their hearts' desire until they agitate the whole community with you and with us also, in grief and affliction and great disturbance and much speech full of every sin. Is it not written in the letters, and have I not sent to you many times, 'Do not act alone at all without her who is appointed with you'. And why did you not ... *4 lines* ... to take care of those who are weak in their feet and also their bodies. Why have you sent to us without her, or why did you speak alone with the elder appointed

[3] Lit. : 'man-pleasing'. [4] Or : 'he'. [5] Cf. Rom. 16. 18.

for the gate amongst you, and she did not come with you? Is it not written in the letters, and have I not sent to you many times, 'Do not let any woman go out to the gate alone'. Or do the elders appointed amongst you not know that it is thus written in the letters, or have I not told them many times very forcefully ... to you ... not to [speak] ... woman ... either the brethren who are inside the community with you, or some who have come from outside, except those two together[6]. And why did they not fear the words of God and his commandments? Or why do you despise them in your transgression? Are they not the commandments of life, in that he who shall * forsake them with us and with you shall * p. 129
die even as also formerly? Or is it not a disgrace for you according to our way of life to cause one of you

CODEX **F**

[Fragment 40] *FRAGMENT*

I. **1.** [And] the godloving presbyter, the archimandrite, he ... champion [of] the truth ... *Unknown number of lines missing* ... crucify him. **2.** He goes round into every place preaching the word of God, but he came to you in order that he might enjoy your fountains which pour forth sweetness, and return to us forthwith to the east[1], when he was given to drink from the rivers, yours and his, which pour forth living water.

[Fragment 41]
TO THE DIGNITARIES AND PEOPLE OF THE VILLAGES

A letter of our godloving father, Apa Besa, to the people that live in the villages at the time when they began to fight with one another, urging them not to war with each other.

I. **1.** Besa the most humble writes to the presbyters, and the deacons, and the administrators, and the headmen, and all the people that live in the villages, greetings in the Lord. **2.** Whereas

[6] I.e. two nuns.

[1] Or possibly : 'source', though this meaning of the Greek word is attested only for the plural, cf. H. G. LIDDELL and R. SCOTT, *A Greek-English Lexicon*, Oxford, 1951, p. 123 b.

we have been informed concerning you that you prepare yourselves to fight with one another for naught over a piece of wood and, when we had heard, our heart was deeply grieved. First then, * p. 130 such a thing is not * fitting for us, we being Christians, nor again is it pleasing to God, nor is it pleasing to men. **3.** Therefore, we have considered that it was right that we should write to you as a brother, entreating you through God and our Lord Jesus Christ that you should spare your own souls and your bodies, and remove yourselves from these unlawful things which God and men hate. **4.** For also it is thus written, 'It is not right for a servant of the Lord to fight'[1]. For such things are not for men who say, 'We are Christians'. And again the holy apostle says, 'Neither brawlers, nor revilers, shall inherit the kingdom of God'[2]. **5.** More especially, if there is a murder, woe to the man through whom it shall occur. He shall be liable to the judgement of God[3]. For also our reverend; holy father has written to some, fighting with one another, thus ... *Unknown number of lines missing* ... is [the] devil. **6.** And there is no advantage on any side but only grief and loss. And do not think that I hate you saying these things to you, but I love you as a brother, that you may escape the judgement of God in the place to which we shall go and the punishments which are executed on all murderers, as it is said, 'He who shall shed the [blood] of man, [instead shall his] be shed'[4]. ... *Unknown number of lines missing* ... **7.** [Cease from] your wickednesses, learn to do good[5], perhaps God will have mercy upon us and send us the yearly inundation and take from us all the tribulations. Or perhaps, indeed, there is no such remembrance in our heart because many are they who grieve

CODEX G

[Fragment 42] *TO SINFUL NUNS*

* p. 131 I. **1.** * you will not put away from you the deceitful counsel and the evil fetters. If I come to you in anger, I shall not spare you as formerly, according to the word of the apostle, 'If I come I

1 II Tim. 2. 24. 2 Cf. I Cor. 6. 10. 3 Cf. Mt. 5. 21. 4 Cf. Gen. 9. 6.
5 Is. 1. 16-17.

shall not spare you even once more'[1]. I will not number myself with the apostles, being weak in my dilatoriness. By no means! **2.** But I know that God will ask me concerning you, for it is for me to instruct you by the words which I write to you in letters that each one of you should forsake her wickedness and her hostility towards her neighbour. **3.** But it is not for me boldly to come to you in person on account of this matter to speak with you mouth to mouth and to see you face to face, except in a great matter of difficulty which gains importance from God. **4.** Therefore I said, 'If I come I shall not spare you even once more'[2]. For I often think that God has been angry with me because of my timidity concerning you. For I did not act in accordance with that which receives confirmation in my heart through faith, while our reverend father yet was, who has not yet been long dead. **5.** Moreover, he is not satisfied with me now, because I forbear with you who are turned away and cast out from the sphere of the word which is written, 'Follow after peace with everyone, and the sanctification in everything without which no one shall see the Lord'[3]. **6.** And I tell you that, in accordance with the amount of my timidity which is in me from God, even as my spirit is overwhelmed with compassion within me whenever God wills, though I get no thanks, so also he gives resolution into my heart at the time when he wills to do so. **7.** Let us pay attention to that which Eze[kiel] has said

CODEX **H**

[Fragment 43] *ON FAVOURITISM*

* exchange hands for her completely in what is choice, and also for you to give to her what is largest and more. But if it is this one who has come to receive, you stretch out your hand to what is small and very little to give it to her, like the miserable ones. But truly, you and this one for whom you have exchanged hands are wretches in the place where each of you shall be judged according to her works without favour[1], as it is written[2]. Abominations ... *At least* * p. 132

[1] Cf. II Cor. 13. 2. [2] Cf. II Cor. 13. 2. [3] Cf. Heb. 12. 14.

[1] Cf. I Pet. 1. 17. [2] It is possible that some extra letters (not more than 4) followed in the text.

2 lines ... for them to take what is great, whether it is a loaf or whether it is another thing to eat, in order that they may give it into the hand of the one whom they think to be she. And if it is not she but rather this one who has come to receive, then you set aside what is large or choice and take instead what is small or little, to give it into the hand of the one towards whom your affection is not. And when she ... *At least 4 lines* ... when you found that this was not she whom you love in your fleshly desire but rather she whom you hate, because the love in your heart is not perfect in your distribution. And thus this one goes into her house weeping and deploring you. But that one goes into her house rejoicing and blessing you vainly. But also others [among] the daughters ... *At least 3 lines* ... in the place where you give you did not give it, and you give to them until they are satisfied and exceed greatly. If you are not ashamed when I say these things to
* p. 133 you, then there is no Spirit of God in you. * If you do not repent over the things you have done, then no one will have compassion upon you. And if you are not ashamed when I say these things, then I am a wretched man. And if your

CODEX I

[Fragment 44] *ON FORSAKING SINFULNESS*

I. **1**. vengeance on him, according to the vengeance of my wrath lest you perish with him at the same time. **2**. Who shall not say among all the wise men from the prophets and the apostles and our holy father, by whose mouth God bore witness to us, 'I speak to you from one end of the earth to the other'. **3**. Whether man or woman, whether small or great, you shall proclaim more than these things which I have spoken to you in the fire and the worm[1] and every tribulation, according to the things which I have [said] and heard [in] great mournings [in] the place where they are imprisoned. **4**. Now therefore, our beloved brethren, while we are in the body we are able to heal ourselves if we take (medicine), and so God and his Christ wish us to do. Therefore, let us put away these jealousies, these hatreds, these quarrels, and these

[1] Cf. Is. 66. 24, Mk. 9. 48.

contentions from us, for not only shall we not profit by them on the day of our need, but they are harmful to us before God in the place to which we shall go. **5.** Now how after these ... *2 lines* ... from the [devil] and his jealousies, [and] his hatreds, [and] all his impious deeds, shall we not perish with him in the wrath wherewith God and his Christ shall destroy him? **6.** For the words which I heard from you, I read [2] them and I knew them to be full of jealousy, and hatred, and strife, and deceit, and malignity; and whisperers, and slanderers, haters of God, despisers, proud, boasters, seekers after evil [3], according to * the things which the apostle has said from of old. **7.** What shall I say to you? For my wretched self does not forget him who works with you enviously and you work with him very foolishly. Do you make God truly contented with you in your works? And do you gladden the heart of my father and my holy fathers in the place where they are? **8.** What indeed shall you do except jealousy, and hatred, and strife, though you are quite without anxiety, for you have a surfeit of bread and good things.

* p. 134

2 Or : 'announced'. 3 Cf. Rom. 1. 29-30.

INDEX OF REFERENCES AND CITATIONS

A. BIBLICAL

Proverbs

Jeremiah

Baruch

Lamentations

Ezekiel

Daniel (0)

Matthew

B. OTHERS

[1] S collection of 7 letters; E collection of 20 letters.

INDEX OF PROPER NAMES

INDEX OF SUBJECTS

CONTENTS

PRINTED ON PERMANENT PAPER • IMPRIME SUR PAPIER PERMANENT • GEDRUKT OP DUURZAAM PAPIER - ISO 9706

N.V. PEETERS S.A., WAROTSTRAAT 50, B-3020 HERENT